Prince William and Duchess Kate

by Jenny MacKay

LUCENT BOOKS
A part of Gale, Cengage Learning

Farmington Hills, Mich • San Francisco • New York • Waterville, Maine
Meriden, Conn • Mason, Ohio • Chicago

LIBRARY OF CONGRESS CATALOGING-IN-PUBLICATION DATA

MacKay, Jenny, 1978-
Prince William and Duchess Kate / by Jenny MacKay.
pages cm. -- (People in the news)
Includes bibliographical references and index.
ISBN 978-1-4205-1237-3 (hardcover)
1. William, Prince, Duke of Cambridge, 1982- 2. Catherine, Duchess of Cambridge, 1982- 3. Royal couples--Great Britain--Biography. 4. Princes--Great Britain--Biography. 5. Princesses--Great Britain--Biography. I. Title.
DA591.A45W55549 2015
941.086'10922--dc23
[B]
2014048359

Lucent Books
27500 Drake Rd.
Farmington Hills, MI 48331

ISBN-13: 978-1-4205-1237-3

Printed in the United States of America
1 2 3 4 5 6 7 19 18 17 16 15

Contents

Fame and celebrity are alluring. People are drawn to those who walk in fame's spotlight, whether they are known for great accomplishments or for notorious deeds. The lives of the famous pique public interest and attract attention, perhaps because their experiences seem in some ways so different from, yet in other ways so similar to, our own.

Newspapers, magazines, and television regularly capitalize on this fascination with celebrity by running profiles of famous people. For example, television programs such as *Entertainment Tonight* devote all their programming to stories about entertainment and entertainers. Magazines such as *People* fill their pages with stories of the private lives of famous people. Even newspapers, newsmagazines, and television news frequently delve into the lives of well-known personalities. Despite the number of articles and programs, few provide more than a superficial glimpse at their subjects.

Lucent's People in the News series offers young readers a deeper look into the lives of today's newsmakers, the influences that have shaped them, and the impact they have had in their fields of endeavor and on other people's lives. The subjects of the series hail from many disciplines and walks of life. They include authors, musicians, athletes, political leaders, entertainers, entrepreneurs, and others who have made a mark on modern life and who, in many cases, will continue to do so for years to come.

These biographies are more than factual chronicles. Each book emphasizes the contributions, accomplishments, or deeds that have brought fame or notoriety to the individual and shows how that person has influenced modern life. Authors portray their subjects in a realistic, unsentimental light. For example, Bill Gates—cofounder of the software giant Microsoft—has been instrumental in making personal computers the most vital tool of the modern age. Few dispute his business savvy, his perseverance, or his technical expertise, yet critics say he is ruthless in his dealings with competitors and driven more by his desire to maintain Microsoft's dominance in the computer industry than by an interest in furthering technology.

In these books, young readers will encounter inspiring stories about real people who achieved success despite enormous obstacles. Oprah Winfrey—one of the most powerful, most watched, and wealthiest women in television history—spent the first six years of her life in the care of her grandparents while her unwed mother sought work and a better life elsewhere. Her adolescence was colored by pregnancy at age fourteen, rape, and sexual abuse.

Each author documents and supports his or her work with an array of primary and secondary source quotations taken from diaries, letters, speeches, and interviews. All quotes are footnoted to show readers exactly how and where biographers derive their information and provide guidance for further research. The quotations enliven the text by giving readers eyewitness views of the life and accomplishments of each person covered in the People in the News series.

In addition, each book in the series includes photographs, annotated bibliographies, timelines, and comprehensive indexes. For both the casual reader and the student researcher, the People in the News series offers insight into the lives of today's newsmakers—people who shape the way we live, work, and play in the modern age.

The Fascination with Royalty

United States citizens live in a republic, where people elect leaders based on merit rather than birthright. Monarchs such as kings, queens, emperors, and sultans may seem to belong to faraway places or long-ago times; however, the governmental structure of monarchy is still very much alive in the world. Twenty-six reigning sovereigns serve as heads of state of forty-three nations. Of these, the monarchy of Britain is the largest and best known, holding a place of honor not just in the United Kingdom—which comprises the nations of England, Scotland, Wales, and Northern Ireland—but in Canada, Australia, New Zealand, the Bahamas, and several smaller nations, totaling sixteen countries in all. As former British colonies, these nations have close ties to England, and the reigning British monarch holds a place of honor, respect, and celebrity for their citizens.

The United States, too, began as a British colony, and its citizens have always paid attention to what is happening in the British royal family. In 1980, American curiosity about the British royals was boosted when Prince Charles, firstborn son of the reigning queen, Elizabeth II, and heir to the British throne, married a beautiful, stylish, and charismatic young woman named Diana Spencer. Awareness of British royalty became fashionable like never before. In the wake of Diana's fame, her and Charles's two sons, William and Harry, found themselves growing up in a media maelstrom. Americans, like much of the rest of the world, never tired of news about the royal family.

Charles and Diana's love story was not quite the fairy tale people had hoped it would be, however. Their failed marriage and the later tragedy of Diana's death in 1997 left a void in the media. Reporters turned their attention to the two royal sons, especially William, who was directly in line to take the throne after his father. He had grown into a handsome teenager, and it became increasingly obvious that eventually, William would choose some lucky young lady and make her a princess. The woman he found came from an unexpected background. She had no ties to royalty; nevertheless, her beauty and character stirred the heart of Prince William and the rest of the world. Their love story unfolded like a fairy tale, and their wedding was one of the most-watched televised events of human history. They had rocketed to celebrity status around the world. Says Katie Nicholl, royal family biographer and correspondent for ABC News: "They are royals. This is a real live prince and princess."[1]

William and Kate live a life of wealth and privilege, but at times they also see themselves as nothing more than college sweethearts who got married and had a baby. Their casual, down-to-earth, everyday approach to life has redefined the world's expectations of how royals should live. They are the king and queen in waiting. They are the Prince and Princess of Wales, the Duke and Duchess of Cambridge, and the future of the British royal family. They are among the most photographed people in the world. They are also simply known as Will and Kate, two ordinary people who found love despite, not because of, William's inheritance of royalty and fame.

Chapter 1

William the Wombat

In London on the evening of June 21, 1982, a baby boy took his first breath in a small delivery room in the maternity ward of St. Mary's Hospital. The happy event—attended by doctors, nurses, and a proud father—was not much different than the arrival of other babies born there that day. The presence of security guards stationed quietly in the hallway did not interfere with bustling hospital staff tending to an overjoyed new mother and her healthy child. Within hours of the baby's delivery, however, the street outside the hospital filled with a crowd of well-wishers. The new mother was Princess Diana, wife of Prince Charles, the firstborn son of Her Majesty Queen Elizabeth II, and the couple's new baby was first in line after his father to occupy the British throne one day. It was a humble beginning to a life of privilege, duty, tragedy, and triumph.

A Royal Start in Life

The new prince was not the queen of England's first grandchild, but he was the most important. Longstanding royal customs dictated that a firstborn royal son would become king upon the death of the reigning king or queen. Queen Elizabeth II had become the monarch in 1952 at age twenty-five because she had had no brothers when her father, King George VI, died. The queen had four children of her own, and her firstborn, Charles, would be her successor. In 1982, Prince Charles's own firstborn son became second in line to take the throne. The arrival of this high-status child was a tremendous occasion. Centuries of tradition bestowed great wealth and privilege on the baby, along with expectations and duties he would never be able to ignore.

Despite being steeped in elaborate customs, Princess Diana had little in common with royal British mothers who had raised princes before her. When she learned she was going to have a child, the headstrong twenty-year-old began to redefine how a British prince should be raised. From the moment she stepped

Diana, Princess of Wales (center) holds her son Prince William at Buckingham Palace after William's christening ceremony in 1982. Also pictured (clockwise from left) Queen Elizabeth II, Prince Charles, Prince Philip, and the Queen Mother, Prince William's great-grandmother.

The Many Names of a Prince

Choosing a baby's name is a task all new parents face, but when that baby is in line to inherit a throne, the job can be daunting. It took Charles and Diana, Prince and Princess of Wales, a full week after the birth of their first son in June 1982 to announce what the new royal baby would be called. His first names were picked from his ancestors or from former kings. The prince would be called by the first of his names, William, but if and when he one day became king, he could choose whatever first name he liked best—King William, King Arthur, King Philip, or King Louis. As for William's surname, British royals customarily use a place as their last name. Since William's father Charles was the Prince of Wales, William took the surname Wales, which was simpler to say than the official last name of his line of the royal family, Mountbatten-Windsor, after his grandmother, Queen Elizabeth II of Windsor, and his grandfather, Prince Philip Mountbatten.

Diana, who strongly favored a modern, everyday name for her son, often called him Wills. The one-syllable nickname stuck with him through his university years and beyond.

out of the hospital cradling her baby in her arms, she carved her own traditions. British princes had always been born in castles, for one thing, but Diana had chosen to give birth in a modern medical facility. "The decision for a hospital birth was popular with the media and the public," says biographer Joann F. Price. "For the media, access to the princess and the heir was immediate because neither mother nor baby was sequestered behind castle or palace walls. For the public, it was a sure sign that this baby would instantly be introduced to and then raised in a world vastly different from that of his family and ancestors."[2]

The nontraditional birth location was just the beginning of a streak of trendsetting. Diana saw herself as a mother first, a member of the royal family second. The former kindergarten teacher adored children and had very strong opinions about raising her own. Once Diana decided to do something a certain way, not even the queen herself could change the princess's mind.

The royal baby, officially named Prince William Arthur Philip Louis, was christened in the same white lace gown his ancestor King Edward VII had worn during his own christening in 1842. The new prince had access to nearly every privilege in the kingdom. Diana hired royal decorators to outfit his nursery and personal maids to wash and fold his laundry. A nanny who specialized in caring for the infants of wealthy families rocked him and cooed to him. Above all, however, Diana wanted time alone with her child. He was a prince, but he was also her little boy. She and Charles strived to create a home filled with toys, laughter, and love—a home like any non-prince might have.

Early Glimpses of the Prince

When he was just nine months old, William accompanied Charles and Diana on a six-week visit to Australia. This was highly unusual. Babies of William's importance usually stayed home with nannies when their parents traveled. Royal photographer Arthur Edwards recalls the palace's response: "They said, 'Well, no, royal babies don't go on these tours.' She (Diana) said, 'William doesn't go, I don't go.'"[3] Taking William with her overseas was one of Diana's ways of setting her parenting style apart from that of Queen Elizabeth II, who had often left Charles and her three other children at home for months at a time during the course of fulfilling her royal duties abroad. Diana wanted a much closer relationship with her own son.

Meanwhile, Charles, a product of royal upbringing in which parents typically interacted with their children from a distance, was often torn between the royal customs he was used to and the contrary wishes of his young wife. Early in William's life, Charles and Diana started to drift apart. Despite the love each had for William, their disagreements only worsened as he grew.

A Brother for William

Two years after the fanfare of William's arrival, Diana discovered that she and Charles were to have a second baby. On September 15, 1984, the royal family welcomed another son, Prince Henry Charles Albert David. His parents called him Harry, and by that time they had also given his older brother a nickname—Wombat, after a popular Australian animal. Harry and Wombat grew up playing army games together at their two main homes, Kensington Palace in London and a country home called Highgrove that was surrounded by parks and trails for horseback riding. Kensington Palace was their mother's favored place. Charles preferred Highgrove. The young princes split their time between homes, and often between parents, too.

A Normal Life for a Future Monarch

It was important to Diana that her sons should have the same experiences as did children who were not royalty. When William was three years old, he was enrolled in Mrs. Mynor's Nursery School, a private preschool in London. British princes were typically educated at home, in part to keep them away from the prying eyes of reporters and photographers, but Diana had other ideas for her sons. In September 1985, William dressed himself for his first day of school and went off to learn alongside children who were not princes and princesses—and who were too young to know that he was one.

As William got older, his peers began to realize that he was different, and so did he. The bodyguards who followed him everywhere were one sign of his importance. "William would tell other children, 'If you don't do what I want, I'll have you arrested!'"[4] reports royal-family journalist Peter Archer. William also discovered that many adults were reluctant to tell him "no." During his preschool years, William could be stubborn and bossy. He threw tantrums and often acted like a spoiled child. As the firstborn in his family, he was even different from his brother. Young William wanted to be a policeman and protect his mother from harm, but Harry was quick to dash

Prince William (left) arrives for his first day at Mrs. Mynor's Nursery School in London, England, accompanied by his mom and dad, in September 1985.

his bossy brother's hopes: "Oh no you can't, you've got to be king!"[5]

From Tantrums to Duties

As the years passed, William's behavior gave way to a more mature and thoughtful outlook. He began to understand that being a prince was not about always getting his way; quite the opposite. He discovered that his life was already planned out for him, and in many ways, his freedom was limited.

The pressures of living in the public eye were as much a burden for William as for Charles and Diana. The royal couple argued often and became cold and distant toward each other. William and Harry found that more and more of their time was split between London, where they did city things with their mother, such as shopping and listening to pop music, and Highgrove, where they hunted and rode horses with Charles.

Princess Diana and Princes Harry and William enjoy an amusement ride at Thorpe Park, a theme park in England. Diana was adamant that her sons enjoy normal activities as much as possible.

Both parents loved the princes, but the parents no longer loved each other.

The press was infatuated with every detail of the troubled royal marriage. Whenever the family made public outings or traveled together, photographers were never far away. If Diana gave Charles a dirty look, it was sure to turn up on the front page of a newspaper. William disliked the reporters and

prying cameras that made his parents' private issues a public spectacle.

Despite the ever-present press, Diana still tried to give her sons the same experiences other children had. "She made sure that they experienced things like going to the cinema, queuing [lining] up to buy a McDonalds, going to amusement parks, those sorts of things that were experiences that they could share with their friends,"[6] says Patrick Jephson, Princess Diana's former chief of staff. William learned to enjoy these everyday experiences, and more than anything, normalcy was what the prince began to want.

Schools Fit for a Prince

When William outgrew preschool, Charles and Diana enrolled him in a private London elementary school called Wetherby, where he spent three years. Then, at age eight, he left the comfort and privacy of his parents' city and country homes to attend Ludgrove, a boarding school for boys that was an hour's drive from London. At the 130-acre (53ha) private campus, surrounded by parks and woodlands, William lived in a dormitory room with four fellow students. He attended classes on weekdays and church services on Sundays. He took up water polo in his free time, a sport at which he soon excelled.

Even though his personal security guards always hovered nearby, William was largely accepted as just another boy at Ludgrove. His life there sheltered him from his parents' crumbling marriage. William knew even less about the state of their relationship than most of the kingdom did, because Ludgrove's principal often kept newspapers away from the students so William would not have to read about his quarreling parents. It was an unhappy surprise when Charles and Diana drove to Ludgrove one afternoon in December 1992 to tell ten-year-old William and eight-year-old Harry, who by then was also a student at Ludgrove, that they were separating.

The news was difficult for both princes. Not only did they face the turmoil of a broken family, but rumors of their parents' extramarital affairs had also made the divorce a royal scandal.

The press exploited every detail. Wherever the royal family went, paparazzi—freelance photographers who get paid for candid photos of celebrities—were close behind. Photographers especially hounded Diana, whose beauty, kindness, and grace had earned her worldwide fame.

William had never been a fan of the press, but in the aftermath of his parents' divorce, his disdain for reporters and photographers led him to shun the public eye. During a cruise the princes took with their mother in 1997, the paparazzi became such a nuisance that Diana shouted from the cruise-ship deck, "William is freaked out."[7] William spent most of the vacation below deck to avoid the photographers altogether. "I don't like attention," he has said. "I like to keep my private life private."[8] More than ever during his parents' separation, William yearned to be just like everyone else.

One Step Closer to the Castle

William finished at Ludgrove in 1995, and at age thirteen he was accepted into Eton College, a prestigious boarding school for young men that was founded by King Henry VI in 1440. Eton was just outside of London in the county of Berkshire and near Windsor Castle, where William sometimes went on weekends to visit his grandmother, the queen. Elizabeth was very close to her grandson, and William often sought her advice about dealing with the pressures of endless public attention. To help him cope, Elizabeth struck a deal with the press that they were not to take photos of either William or Harry while the princes were at school. In exchange, the palace agreed to give the press regular updates about the princes and arranged for William and Harry to make at least one public appearance with photo opportunities each semester.

Despite the queen's request that the press keep its distance, Eton was much more open to the world than Ludgrove had been, and this made it difficult for William to feel like he was just another student. He decorated the walls of his dormitory room with posters of supermodels just like many of his peers did; however, his window, which overlooked a public street,

Prince William is photographed on his first day at his boarding school, Eton College. The royal family agreed to give the press one public appearance per semester with photo opportunities.

was outfitted with bulletproof glass, and wherever he went, his protection detail was never far away. When William was on his way to a match to compete in soccer, rugby, or his favorite sport, water polo, crowds lined the paths of the school to catch a glimpse of the prince.

Eton was also open to all the newspapers, magazines, and tabloids that publicized the royal family's personal life. In November 1995, just a few months after William's arrival at the school, he was deeply embarrassed when Diana gave a sit-down television interview and exposed private details of her and Charles's extramarital relationships. William felt betrayed, and for a while, he would not speak to his mother.

The prince did his best to ignore the royal gossip by burying himself in sports, schoolwork, and the friendships he made at Eton. He wanted no special treatment in the classroom or on the sports field and expected to be held to the same standards as everyone else. He was respected and popular among his peers, and his life at Eton was as close to normal as a teenage prince could expect to find. Then a tragedy struck that put both William and Harry in the spotlight, not just in England but around the world.

The Loss of a Princess

The bad news came at the end of summer 1997. William and Harry had spent August with their father at Balmoral Castle in Scotland while Diana vacationed with friends. She spent the end of August in Paris, France, with Dodi Fayed, a wealthy Egyptian film producer she had been dating that summer. On Saturday, August 31, Diana spoke to William, then aged fifteen, on the phone and said she was flying back to London the following morning. The princes went to bed, eager to spend the next couple of days with their mother before returning to school for the fall term.

Late that night, Diana and Fayed were passengers in a Mercedes-Benz that was driving too fast through a tunnel in Paris, reportedly trying to escape paparazzi chasing the car on motorcycles. The car's journey ended in a violent crash. Fayed

Prince Philip, Prince William, Earl Spencer, Prince Harry, and Prince Charles (left to right) walk outside Westminster Abbey in the funeral procession for Princess Diana in 1997.

and the driver died at the scene. Diana was pulled from the wreckage and was sped to a Paris hospital. She underwent surgery for massive internal injuries, but her heart stopped in the early morning hours of September 1. She died while her two children slept peacefully in Scotland.

Charles broke the devastating news to his sons the following morning. More than ever, the heartbroken princes felt the pressures of royal duty. They walked behind the coffin that carried Diana's body during a funeral procession attended by a million people. Through it all, they were expected to behave more like steadfast princes than like grieving sons who had just lost their mother. They completed the march with their heads hung in sorrow, but with dry eyes. "William, who has the Windsor ability to keep his emotions hidden, appeared to be remarkably controlled,"[9] says biographer Penny Junor. William's future subjects got a glimpse of the poised, mature young man their prince had grown to be.

A Prince Becomes a Man

William grew very close to his father and brother in the years following Diana's death. He also developed an adventurous spirit combined with a desire to help people in need throughout the world. Diana had devoted much of her life to charitable work, and William wanted to continue that legacy.

In 1999, William entered his final year at Eton. He became a pop, a student supervisor who patrolled the campus to make sure fellow students obeyed rules such as returning to their dormitories before curfew each night. He also mentored Harry, who was now a student at Eton, too. By the following spring, William was narrowing down his top choices in universities. The handsome prince, now more than 6 feet (2m) tall, had a new reputation as one of the world's most famous up-and-coming bachelors, and he had gathered a significant media following.

William had always blamed the paparazzi for his mother's death, however, and still sought to avoid most of the fame that was both a birthright and a burden. "If you're born into it I think it's normal to feel as though you don't really want it,"[10] he said in a television interview. By age eighteen, William had taken to riding around London on a motorcycle, in part because of the freedom of being impossible to recognize while wearing a helmet.

After finishing at Eton, William took a gap year, a break in which to travel and try new things before enrolling in a university. This was something Charles had not done at William's age, but he understood his eldest son's desire to experience the world before settling into university life. Charles arranged for William's gap year to include military training and humanitarian service. Above all, the trip abroad meant William could experience being somewhat anonymous while helping other people.

William traveled to Central and South America, where he participated in grueling military training in a jungle in Belize before spending ten weeks in Chile with a volunteer organization

Dreaming of Africa

William was a teenager when he visited Africa for the first time. The continent's open landscapes and diverse wildlife captivated him. He relished sleeping under the stars and walking through towns and villages where no one knew who he was.

Africa's influence never left William. His twenty-first birthday party at Windsor Castle had the theme "Out of Africa," with guests dressed in animal costumes and the castle decorated with bush scenes and a life-sized elephant made of papier mâché. Africa was the place William would choose to propose to his future wife, and it was the nursery theme for his firstborn child.

In 2005, William became the royal patron of an anti-poaching organization called Tusk. He has since lent his name to the Prince William Award for Conservation in Africa, which honors the work of dedicated conservationists working to preserve Africa's endangered species. "As long as I can put my voice and my support behind people like that, those are the guys, those are the girls who will inspire the next generation," William says. "You want to stand up for what is very vulnerable and what needs protecting." It is one of the ways William uses his fame for good.

Quoted in CNN. *Prince William's Passion: New Father, New Hope*. Documentary. Aired September 15, 2012. Transcript available at http://transcripts.cnn.com/TRANSCRIPTS/1309/15/se.02.html.

called Raleigh International. There, alongside volunteers from all over the world, he helped build roads and teach English to children in an impoverished mountain village. He slept in a sleeping bag on the floor just like his fellow volunteers. Dressed in sweatshirts, jeans, and sandals with socks, William was free to be himself. "I love having no restrictions here," he said during his time in Chile. "There's no one out here chasing me around. It's brilliant."[11]

William took a gap year after Eton in 2000 and volunteered with Raleigh International in the village of Tortel, Chile, where he helped build roads and taught English to children.

During William's gap year, he learned that his final grades from Eton were good enough to get into his top-choice school, the University of St. Andrews in Scotland. In 2001, after months of living without the burden of a title, he returned to Great Britain. Under the unassuming name of William Wales, he prepared for a new phase in his life, one of academics and adulthood—and love.

Chapter 2

Kate the Commoner

In July 1981, Michael and Carole Middleton watched the lavish royal wedding of Prince Charles and Lady Diana Spencer on television from their modest but comfortable home in Bradfield, a quiet village in the rural county of Berkshire about forty-five minutes outside of London. The Middletons were newly married themselves, having celebrated their own wedding at a historic manor house in 1980. Theirs had been elegant for a wedding in the English countryside, but the pomp and ceremony of the royal nuptials in London seemed a world apart.

Carole was a flight attendant for British Airways, an impressive occupation for a young woman whose family did not have the money for a university education. The jet-setting career gave her the opportunity to visit exotic destinations. It also introduced her to Michael Middleton, a flight dispatcher whose job was to make sure flights left on schedule and carried the correct cargo. Whereas Carole's family had little money, Michael's was significantly better off. Carole came from a line of coal miners, factory workers, and other laborers, some of whom had lived in poverty. Many of Michael's ancestors had been successful merchants and businesspeople. His great-grandfather had created a trust fund worth millions of dollars for the education of Middleton descendants, so Michael had been able to attend highly esteemed private schools. His job as a flight dispatcher was prestigious, and he met many flight attendants who were interested in dating him. It was Carole

Kate Middleton's childhood home is in the village of Bradfield Southend, England.

Goldsmith, however, who caught his eye, and the two fell in love.

After their wedding, Carole and Michael wanted to start a family. They purchased a red brick house amid the rolling green hills and country lanes surrounding the village of Bradfield. In 1981, when they learned they were to become parents, Carole left British Airways, choosing motherhood over a traveling career that would take her away from her baby. Even though she missed the excitement of being a flight attendant, she looked forward to raising her first child, since both she and Michael had come from very close families. On the snowy night of January 9, 1982, Carole and Michael welcomed their daughter Catherine Elizabeth into the world—just two months after the royal family had announced that Princess Diana was also pregnant and would give birth to her first child the following summer.

A Girl from Two Countries

West View, the name of Carole and Michael's countryside house, truly felt like a home with the addition of Catherine (who was not called Kate until her teen years). "Catherine was a lovely little baby, cherubic and chubby cheeked and so good," says George Brown, one of the Middletons' former neighbors. "I remember she didn't cry much at all."[12] Having given up the globe-trotting glamour of being a flight attendant, Carole became very involved in home and village life. She made friends with her neighbors, baked treats for community events, and took Catherine to mother-and-child playgroups.

Shortly after Catherine turned one year old, Carole and Michael learned that a second Middleton child was on the way. On September 6, 1983, they welcomed Catherine's little sister Philippa Charlotte, whom they called Pippa for short. Carole often took Catherine on outings while pushing Pippa in a high-end Silver Cross baby carriage made by the same company that has supplied strollers to the royal family's babies since 1877. The expensive baby carriage, the same brand that carried Prince William and Prince Charles, had been one of the Middletons' splurges when they first learned they were to be parents.

Fancy items like a royal-quality baby carriage were not everyday purchases for the Middletons. Although Michael came from a well-to-do family, the majority of his inheritance had been set aside by his relatives to pay for his children's education. For day-to-day expenses, the growing Middleton family depended on Michael's British Airways salary. When Catherine was two years old, Michael was transferred to Amman, the capital city of Jordan, on the eastern border of Israel. In May 1984, the Middletons exchanged their quiet village lifestyle for a two-story urban home in the densely populated hills of a bustling Middle Eastern city.

In Amman, Catherine and Pippa spent many hot summer afternoons in an inflatable pool in their small backyard (called the garden in British idiom), where the Middletons also hosted dinnertime garden parties. Carole enjoyed cooking and would often serve meals for as many as thirty guests. The Middleton's

home in Jordan was a busy and social place for Catherine and Pippa.

Giving her daughters a world-class education was important to Carole, so when Catherine was three, her parents enrolled her in a nursery school within walking distance of their home. Because of Michael's trust fund, education was the one area of the Middletons' life where money was no object, and Catherine's new school was the most expensive in the neighborhood for children aged three to five. She met children from countries such as the United States, Japan, and Indonesia and learned to recite passages from both the Bible and the Koran, the

Amman—the ancient, yet modern capital of Jordan—was home to the Middletons for two and a half years in the 1980s, when Michael Middleton was transferred there for work.

holy book of the religion of Islam. "Kate had a happy childhood here," says Sahira Nabulsi, owner and director of the nursery school. "She took part in all the activities with the other children. We sang songs in Arabic and English."[13]

Catherine also developed a love of art and theater at Assahera. She painted exotic birds and acted in school plays. For two and a half years, the Middletons enjoyed a bustling, multicultural, urban lifestyle, but in 1986, Michael's transfer ended. Catherine, now four, and Pippa, two, returned with their parents to their home in Bradfield, where another upscale private school was already holding a place for Catherine.

Back to School

The Middletons quickly resumed life in their English village, and Catherine began attending St. Andrews, a preparatory school for boys and girls aged three to thirteen. Although she could be shy and quiet, Catherine was quick to try new things and became involved in a variety of pastimes. She took part in Girl Scouts, and as a Brownie she earned merit badges for accomplishments from housekeeping to the arts. She took piano lessons, learned to play the flute, and also enjoyed singing. Her school put on two plays a year, and Catherine had parts in nearly all of them.

Kate Middleton attended St. Andrew's School in Berkshire, England, when her family returned to the United Kingdom from Jordan.

Although she adored the theater, Catherine was nowhere more at home than on the sports field. She was a fast runner, a strong swimmer, and an all-around athlete. Her favorite sports included field hockey, tennis, and netball, which is similar to American basketball. At St. Andrews, she competed on many winning teams and set school records in swimming. Carole and Michael encouraged Catherine to eat extra portions at meals and not to skimp on desserts just to help her growing body keep up with her highly active lifestyle.

A Baby Brother and a Business

Pippa later joined Catherine at St. Andrews, and together the sisters were a formidable force in sports. They were competitive but also very close. Peers nicknamed them Pip (for Pippa) and Squeak (for Catherine) after the two guinea pigs who were school pets. The Middleton family was a familiar fixture at the school and its sporting events and well-liked in town. Their family, however, was about to grow once more. On April 15, 1987, Carole gave birth to her and Michael's third child, James William. They were delighted to finally have a brother for their active girls, and the close-knit family was finally complete.

Even with the Middleton family's education trust fund, private preparatory school for three children was pricey. To help make ends meet, Carole started a new business venture while she was pregnant with James. She had always liked to throw themed birthday parties for her daughters and had a knack for creating clever bags of treats for all the young guests. Carole's friends began asking her to make bags for their own children's parties. Britain had yet to catch on to the trend of birthday treat bags that were a hit in the United States, and Carole had trouble finding inexpensive trinkets to use in party-favor bags. "I was looking for party stuff for my own children's parties," Carole says. "It was impossible to find anything easily in the shops. . . . So I came up with the idea for Party Pieces."[14]

Before long, Carole had a steady stream of local orders for inexpensive children's party supplies. She made bags in her kitchen for a while, then moved her budding business to a remodeled shed in the backyard. The Internet was just becoming popular at the time, and Carole's business-savvy younger brother, Gary Goldsmith, suggested she move her business online to reach more customers. She gave online selling a try in the early 1990s and added more party supplies to her list of offerings, such as themed decorations and party kits. Soon the company was making enough money for Michael to leave his job at British Airways and work for Party Pieces. The mail-order party supply business eventually made them millionaires and secured a prosperous future for their three children.

Secondary School Woes

Catherine so enjoyed St. Andrews that at age nine, she pleaded with her parents to let her board there, meaning she could live there all week long. This added considerably to tuition expenses,

In the 1990s, Carole and Michael Middleton started the online mail-order party supply business Party Pieces, which made them millionaires.

but with the success of Carole's business, the family could afford the boarding option. Living at school during the week gave Catherine even more time to be involved in sports, and on weekends she often brought friends to the Middleton home for Saturday night sleepovers. "I remember camping in the backyard with Catherine and Pippa," says Fiona Beacroft, one of Catherine's childhood friends. "The family are lovely people, very sociable and the house was always filled with laughter."[15]

Catherine thoroughly enjoyed her time at St. Andrews, but at age thirteen, it was time to take off the familiar blue-checkered dress that had been her school uniform for years and move on to the next stage in her education. St. Andrews was a coeducational school, meaning it served both boys and girls, but in the fall of 1995, the Middletons enrolled Catherine at Downe House, an all-girls high school where about 90 percent of the

Was the Future Princess Bullied?

When she was in her early teens, Catherine Middleton faced difficult social relationships at Downe House, the all-girls boarding school she attended. She remained for only half a year before transferring to a different school. Several of her former classmates at Downe report having little memory of Catherine other than that she was thin, pale, and shy, but a few have reported that she endured physical bullying such as having books shoved out of her hands and feces smeared on the sheets of her bed. (The latter probably never happened, since Catherine did not live at the school and therefore would have had no bed for her classmates to sabotage.)

Catherine has not spoken publicly about incidents of bullying in her past, but when she and Prince William got married in 2011, they included the U.K.-based nonprofit organization BeatBullying among the twenty-six charities to which wedding guests and well-wishers could donate. Whether and to what extent the duchess was bullied may never be revealed, but her support of BeatBullying has helped draw attention to the plight of young people whose peers are mean to them.

students were boarders. Catherine, who lived close enough to the campus to come home each evening, chose not to board. This made it difficult for her to form friendships with the live-in girls, who did most of their bonding in the evenings and on weekends. "When she used to go to lunch she would sit down with people and they all used to get up and sit on another table,"[16] says Jessica Hay, one of Catherine's friends.

Catherine was different than most Downe House girls in other ways, too. Having come to the school at age thirteen, she was already an outsider, since most of the girls had started when they were eleven and already knew each other. Catherine was thin and tall for her age. She also was not as outgoing as the other girls and kept to herself much of the time. Even on the sports field, the one place Catherine usually felt she could shine, she was at a disadvantage. The sport she played best was field hockey, but Downe did not have a field hockey team. Its most popular sport was lacrosse, a game Catherine had never played.

Catherine spent a lonely and unhappy autumn at the all-girls school. During the holiday break, her parents decided that Downe House was not the right place for her and that the only way they could make life happier for Catherine was to change schools. Halfway through the year, then, Catherine transferred to Marlborough College in Wiltshire, an hour's drive from her home in Bradfield.

A Fresh Start

Marlborough was a private and pricey co-ed school serving students from age thirteen to eighteen and was known for excellence in academics and sports. Its students boarded for the entire semester, including most weekends. Every weekday included three hours of sports between afternoon classes, making the school a natural home for a girl who had always been most comfortable in a sports uniform.

Kate attended boarding school at Marlborough College, a co-ed school known for strong academic and sports programs.

The social situation was not always easy at Marlborough—during Catherine's first days there, boys held up paper signs rating her looks as a two on a scale from one to ten—but Catherine was comfortable living with boys and girls, having done so for years at St. Andrews. For an athletic and outdoorsy young woman, Marlborough provided plenty of opportunities for sports and also taught its students to befriend and get along with people of either sex.

Catherine made friends among her roommates and classmates. She studied hard in school and particularly enjoyed chemistry, biology, and art. Her skill at sports earned her a coveted spot on Marlborough's winning field hockey team. She also served as co-captain of the tennis team, played netball, and excelled in swimming and high jump.

Pippa joined Catherine at Marlborough the next year, and the Middleton sisters became well known among their peers not just for their athletic prowess but their sophistication, flawless manners, and always fashionable style. "There was always something slightly galling about having your children at school with the Middletons," says the mother of one of Catherine and Pippa's Marlborough classmates. "Every pristine item of clothing would have a beautifully sewn-in name tape, for instance. It was unthinkable that they would end up resorting to marker pen on labels like the rest of us."[17]

Toward the end of Catherine's time at Marlborough, boys were no longer rating her as a two but as a ten. When the sixteen-year-old, now known to her friends as Kate, returned from summer break before her final year, her bright smile, chestnut-colored hair, and athletic build caught the eye of many a male classmate; however, she remained mostly aloof toward these boys, laughing that she had set her sights on the prince. "She would joke, 'There's no one quite like William,'"[18] Hay recalls, although in a television interview years later, Kate denied rumors that she had had posters of the prince on her walls as a teenager. "No, I had the Levis guy on my wall, not a picture of William,"[19] she claimed.

Serious romance was not a priority for Kate when she graduated from Marlborough in the summer of 2000. She was instead focused on getting the most out of her upcoming gap year and making a decision about which university she would attend.

Near Brushes with Royalty

After leaving Marlborough, Kate traveled to Florence, Italy, for a three-month course in art history, which she had decided would be her major at whatever university she chose. Rumors circulated that Prince William, who was also in his gap year, might also come to Italy to study. He ended up doing other things, but Kate was more interested in photographs of Italian buildings anyhow.

Following her months of studying art in Florence, Kate joined the volunteer group Raleigh International and spent twelve weeks

Preparing for the Royal Stage

Catherine Middleton's many childhood interests included music and drama. When she was eleven years old, she played the role of Eliza Doolittle in a school musical production of *My Fair Lady*. In the play, Eliza is a flower vendor who lacks the manners and polished speech of a proper English lady. A language professor takes a bet that he can teach her to dress, speak, and act like a lady so convincingly that she will be able to pass in high society. By the end of the play, the transformed Eliza has indeed become ladylike enough to capture the heart of an upper-class gentleman but not without first teaching the professor a few things about looking deeper than a person's surface.

Playing the lead in a play about climbing from one social class to another, Catherine in some ways seemed to have predicted her own future. She was to face some of the same opinions and prejudices as Eliza; however, Catherine, like the character she played, revealed likeability, a witty sense of humor, and self-confidence, traits that have served her well both on stage and in life.

in southern Chile, starting in January 2001. Had she attended the previous session, which had ended in December, she would have lived in close quarters with Prince William. Instead, he was just leaving Chile when she arrived. "I think a lot of people don't realise there is that common connection there in their pasts,"[20] says Malcolm Sutherland, the instructor who led both Kate's and William's Raleigh International expeditions in Chile.

During her busy gap year, Kate surprised her friends and family with her decision about what university she was planning to attend. She had been leaning toward Oxford Brookes (formerly called the Oxford School of Art) or Edinburgh University, but she changed her mind and decided to attend the University of St. Andrews in Scotland. The prestigious school, the third oldest in the English-speaking world, had a highly rated art history program. Prince William, too, was headed to St. Andrews that fall. Like Kate, he planned to study the history of art. The paths of these two young adults who had so much in common were finally about to cross.

Will and Kate

Late September 2001 was a busy time in Fife, Scotland, home to the six-hundred-year-old University of St. Andrews. Thousands of new and returning students flooded the small town's quaint old streets with the excitement of a new school year. The traditional Freshers Week, an orientation period for new students, was in full swing.

One new student skipped most of the festivities. He had enrolled under the unassuming name of William Wales, but even without the princely title, it was no secret that the heir to the British throne had come to St. Andrews. While his carefree fellow freshers (short for *freshmen*, or first-year students) caroused, William was helping direct the security setup of his dormitory in St. Salvator's Hall and giving a brief interview to reporters eager for a look at the building where the prince would sleep at St. Andrews.

One freshers tradition involved students' dressing in silly costumes and covering each other in shaving cream. Kate Middleton was in the midst of the action, her long brown hair pulled up into pigtails, and her cheeks stained a clownish pink as she grinned beneath a layer of foam. Will, as the prince now wanted to be called, might have joined in the fun as well were it not for the two things that intimidated him most about attending a university—being swarmed by crowds of young people eager to brush shoulders with royalty and having his every move caught on camera.

The press, at the royal family's request, had promised to keep its distance from Will so he could attempt to experience being just another student. Nevertheless, he knew that an embarrassing bout of un-kingly behavior could put his face on the cover of every tabloid in the English-speaking world. Thus, while an anonymous nineteen-year-old Kate Middleton joined foam-covered throngs of partyers, William Wales hid from them. The two fellow freshmen at St. Andrews were leading very different lives, but that was about to change.

Rooms at Sally's

St. Salvator's Hall, called Sally's for short, is one of the oldest residence halls at St. Andrews. It houses two hundred students every year, and its 2001 resident list included both Kate Middleton and William Wales. In the stairwells and hallways and during daily meals in Sally's wood-paneled dining hall, Will and Kate occasionally bumped into each other. Like everyone else on campus, Kate knew who Will was, but he also knew a thing or two about her. She had earned her own bit of fame when she was dubbed by her peers as the prettiest girl at Sally's.

Will and Kate had many classes together, since they both had declared majors in the history of art. Will was one of only a few men in the program, so during lectures he sat in the front row with his baseball cap pulled low over his head to avoid the awkwardness of girls turning around to stare at him in class. He soon discovered that Kate was not like those girls. Reserved and a little shy, she did not seem to notice or care that he was a prince. She treated him just like any other classmate. Will was instantly at ease, and a friendship sprouted. If one of them missed class, the other would share notes. Will regularly invited Kate to sit with him and his friends at their favorite table in the dining hall at Sally's, where she would sometimes join him for a quick breakfast after her morning jog.

Over bowls of granola-like muesli and fresh fruit, the two learned they had many things in common, like their love of art history, their fondness for skiing, and the time they each had spent in Chile the previous year. When Will discovered that Kate

St. Salvator's Hall was the residence of both Prince William and Kate Middleton when they attended the University of St. Andrews.

was an avid swimmer just like he was, he invited her to join him for dips in the pool at the Old Course Hotel just uphill from St. Andrews, where he regularly went to exercise in private. Kate was not troubled by Will's entourage of bodyguards, and she got along well with his friends at Sally's. The two became frequent companions.

Romance was another matter. Will was reluctant around girls and quick to shun those who just wanted to meet him because he was a prince. Nevertheless, he dated several young women during his first year at St. Andrews. Kate had a boyfriend that year, too, a university senior named Rupert Finch. Despite spending a lot of time together, the prince and the prettiest girl at Sally's thought of each other only as friends.

Seeds of Romance

After one semester at St. Andrews, William decided he did not really like it there. When he went home to spend time with his family during the holidays, he told his father he did not want to go back. "He got the blues, which happens," says Andrew Neil, who was head of St. Andrews at the time. "We have a lot of public school boys and girls who get up here, and by November, when the weather gets grey and cold, wish they were back home. William was a long way from home."[21] Will missed his friends in London, and he also decided he did not care much for his art history classes. The university let him switch his major to geography, and after a few indecisive weeks, he agreed to return to campus, at least for the spring semester.

With his new course schedule, Will saw Kate less often. The two friends might have grown apart if it were not for a fashion show a group of St. Andrews students put together as a fundraiser that spring. Will paid £200 (about $310) for a front-row seat. When Kate appeared on the catwalk wearing nothing but a sheer black slip over her underwear, the prince could not look away. "I remember that specific night very well," says Julian Knight, a close friend of Will's. "She wasn't what you would call a risqué girl. . . . And here she was not wearing that much, looking amazing. I think everyone did think, 'Wow, she looks

After his first semester at St. Andrews, William switched his major from art history to geography.

great. She looks amazing. She's beautiful.' And I think he (Prince William) probably looked to her and was pretty impressed as well."[22]

Later than evening, during a party after the show, Will found Kate in the crowd and they spent a lot of time talking. At one point, he leaned in for a kiss. Kate pulled away because she still had a boyfriend, but that night their friendship became something more.

A Year of Independence and Love

Later that spring, Kate's boyfriend, Rupert Finch, graduated from St. Andrews, and their relationship ended. Will seized the opportunity to ask a newly single Kate to move into a flat (the British term for apartment) with him and two other friends during their second year at St. Andrews. Renting his own flat

For his second year at St. Andrews, William asked two friends and Kate to share a flat. This gave him more freedom to shop and cook his own meals as well as be closer to Kate.

had been one of Will's conditions for returning to the university. He disliked residence-hall life. He wanted to shop at a supermarket, cook his own meals, and walk down the street to the neighborhood pub whenever he wanted. Living in an off-campus apartment, he could do those things. Most important, though, he wanted to live with his new love interest.

Kate accepted the invitation, along with their soon-to-be roommates Olivia Bleasdale and Fergus Boyd. Then Kate and Will went separate ways for the summer. Kate took a job as a barmaid, while Will attended the queen's golden jubilee, a celebration of her fiftieth year on the throne. The differences in their two lifestyles were suddenly very obvious. "Sometimes I can't believe the Will I know and Prince William are the same person,"[23] Kate told Pippa. Whether he went by Will or by the title of prince, however, William's heart was already Kate's. They spoke on the phone nearly every day that summer. When it came time to return to school for the fall semester, the four roommates insisted to outsiders that Will and Kate were just friends, but they were clearly much more.

Life at 13A Hope Street

Will, Kate, and their roommates each paid equal shares of the monthly rent for their flat and divided up chores like shopping, cooking, cleaning, and taking out the garbage. The prince received no favoritism, and he did not want it any other way. When it was Will's turn to cook meals, he revealed that the culinary arts were not his specialty. Kate, who had spent plenty of time in her family's kitchen growing up, frequently stepped in to salvage dinner.

Prince William played water polo for St. Andrews. Although their relationship was still secret, Kate was always at his sporting events to cheer him on.

The college sweethearts kept their increasingly serious relationship hidden from all but their closest friends, but wherever Kate or Will went, the other was usually nearby. Although they made a pact never to hold hands in public, the two were seen walking together around town and campus, and when Will played in sports matches, Kate was often on the sidelines cheering him on.

In their third year at St. Andrews, William and Kate moved to a new home, a cottage-style house with its own garden and grounds that were perfect for private walks and picnics. They also took a skiing trip in March 2004 at a resort called Klosters in Switzerland, and for the first time in public, William stole a kiss from Kate. Naturally, the press was not far away, and as soon as the tabloids and newspapers could be printed, the secret was out: the prince had a girlfriend.

Some women at St. Andrews regarded Kate with curiosity or jealousy, but Kate saw it differently. Reportedly, when a friend told her she was lucky to be with William, Kate replied, "He's lucky to be going out with me."[24] "According to another acquaintance," says biographer Christopher Andersen, "Kate offered something 'none of the other girls had. . . . It's hard to put your finger on it, but so many of those other beautiful girls don't know when to shut up and listen, and she did.'"[25] To the friends who knew them best, Will and Kate seemed a perfect match.

Farewell to University Life

Living together at St. Andrews gave Will and Kate something few other British royal couples have ever had—time to get to know each other as ordinary people. In June 2005, however, their years of relative normalcy came to an end. Will graduated from the university with a degree in geography, and Kate with a degree in art history. Both walked across the stage in the same formal graduation robes, but little else in their lives would ever be quite the same again.

One sign of the changes to come was the presence of royalty in the audience. Queen Elizabeth II attended the ceremony to see her grandson graduate, and of course, Prince Charles was

Fashion Twins

The moment photographers captured the image of William kissing Kate Middleton on a Swiss ski slope was the beginning of a lifetime of fashion scrutiny for the previously unknown young woman. Not since Princess Diana had a British prince's love interest so enchanted the world. Kate's fashion choices appeared in newspaper and magazine photos around the globe, inspiring new style fads seemingly as fast as she could change clothes. Images of Diana were soon resurrected and placed next to photos of Kate whenever the two wore anything similar. If Kate pulled on jeans and a blazer, photos surfaced of Diana in the same. From the fabrics and necklines of their evening gowns to the colors of their skirt suits, from their ski coats and gloves to the angle of the tilt on their fanciest hats, fashion details between the two women were endlessly compared. After William proposed to Kate with the engagement ring that had been his mother's, even the resulting engagement photos were eerily similar to Charles and Diana's. Where Kate differed most from Diana, however, was her confident smile. Diana had often been called Shy Di, but Kate seemed to step into the fashion limelight with ease and pride.

there, too. Will's graduation also marked the end of the royal family's agreement with the press not to intrude on his privacy or follow him around. Photographers would once again be a fixture in the prince's life, and anyone close to him was a potential target. Plenty of photographers wanted snapshots of William's pretty girlfriend, and rumors were already swirling about how serious their relationship really was. Kate Middleton was soon to be a frequent name in news headlines around the world.

Following the graduation ceremony, William gave the press a statement: "I have been able to lead as 'normal' a student life as I could have hoped for, and I am very grateful."[26] It was time, however, for the prince and his girlfriend to step out of small-town Scotland and into the public eye.

Time Apart

After graduating from St. Andrews, Kate started receiving invitations to major royal events, such as Prince Charles's wedding to Camilla Parker Bowles. "I was quite nervous about meeting William's father," Kate says, but "he was very, very welcoming, very friendly, it couldn't have gone easier really for me."[27] Will also spent time with the Middletons and enjoyed their casual, friendly, and close-knit family life. "I get on really well with them," he says. "I've felt really a part of the family and I hope that Kate's felt the same with my family."[28]

In spite of the acceptance from both of their families, however, the relationship was not easy for the young couple. Many people began to question the prince's romantic choice. In a country entrenched in centuries-old royal traditions, some said that Kate's middle-class upbringing was not good enough. "When Kate was established as William's serious girlfriend, whispers abounded . . . that Carole Middleton, whose forebears were coal miners and laborers and who herself ran a company selling party favors, was far too common to be the mother of a future Queen,"[29] says writer Emma Garman.

Kate, who had moved into her own apartment after graduating from St. Andrews, faced a constant barrage of photographers every time she stepped out of her door. She held down different jobs, including working as an accessories buyer for a clothing chain called Jigsaw and later joining the Middleton family business as a website and catalog designer and photographer. She also followed the queen's advice to find a charitable cause and spent time with young patients at a children's hospice. Nothing Kate did, however, could quell the rumors that she was a social climber waiting around in hope of marrying the prince. Many began to think it was a vain hope. The prince himself, when asked about marriage in 2005 at age twenty-two, told the press, "I don't want to get married until I'm at least 28 or maybe 30."[30] Kate's attachment to William, despite his ap-

Prince William takes part in the army's Regular Commissions Board selection process in 2005, enabling him to join the army the next year.

parent reluctance to pop the question, earned her the unkind nickname Waity Katie.

Will, meanwhile, joined his younger brother, Harry, at the Royal Military Academy Sandhurst (usually referred to as simply Sandhurst), in January 2006 to begin forty-eight weeks of officer's training. Royal policy would not allow him to participate on actual battlefields because he was second in line for the throne, but he had decided he wanted a career as a helicopter pilot for the British Royal Air Force. His training kept him away from Kate for the better part of a year and put added strain on their already difficult relationship.

Prince in the Trenches

The reigning king or queen serves as the head of the British armed forces. Prince William, like his father, Charles, before him, was expected to undergo military officer training to prepare him for that eventual role. When he entered the officer-training program at the royal military academy in 2006, William was treated no differently than his 270 fellow recruits. Known as Officer Cadet Wales, he polished boots, ironed shirts, did all his own laundry, and suffered painful blisters from running in boots. He cleaned lavatories, was yelled at by officers, and spent miserable winter nights trekking through miles of wilderness on an empty stomach.

When the grueling forty-four-week training period ended in December 2006, William graduated from Sandhurst with the rank of lieutenant. Throughout the demanding training program, he had displayed leadership, toughness, and a refusal to give up, qualities that are called for in a military officer and equally so in a king.

The Breakup

In the spring of 2007, William, now an officer in the army, received a short break from his military commitments. He chose to spend it with friends in London rather than with Kate. Photographs of the prince at bars and nightclubs with his arms around pretty girls circulated in newspapers and tabloids. The public took the photos to mean the prince had developed a wandering eye and was not ready to settle down.

When Will's breakup with Kate was announced in April 2007, it did not come as a surprise to many. Kate Middleton was simply out of her league, some people said. Others believed the university romance had withered under the pressures of adult life, as often happens with young love. The split was more complicated than that, however. The prince had seen firsthand the pressures royal life could put on a marriage, especially one that began too soon. His mother, Diana, had been twenty years old when she and Charles were engaged after dating just six months, and their marriage had rarely been a happy one. Will seemed wary of making a mistake by rushing into marriage before he and Kate were ready. "We were both very young," he later said about the breakup. "It was very much [about] trying to find our own way and we were growing up."[31]

If Kate was devastated, she scarcely showed it. She spent some time at her family's home, was seen at nightclubs with handsome men, and joined a women's rowing team for charity. The press missed none of it, and neither did the prince. Within months, Will and Kate were back together at the summer concert he and Harry had organized to commemorate the tenth anniversary of Diana's death. The couple's love had survived its greatest test to date.

Betrothed at Last

As soon as Will and Kate had gotten back together, everyone expected to hear news of an engagement. Privately, the two had decided that they *would* marry but that they were in no rush.

Kate Middleton shows off her sapphire engagement ring at a press conference at St. James Palace on November 16, 2010.

"I'm trying to learn from lessons done in the past,"[32] Will said, referring to the whirlwind romances of his parents and other royal ancestors that had resulted in unhappy unions. For years, the public speculated about when the patient prince would propose, but the announcement did not come.

Finally, in October 2010, during a private vacation at a remote log-cabin resort in Rutundu, Kenya, Africa, William presented Kate with the sapphire engagement ring his father had given to his mother. Not even the lodge owners had any idea that their rustic cabin would go down in history as the site where a future king of England proposed to his bride. Kate and Will both signed the resort's guest book, Will writing, "Look forward to next time, soon I hope."[33] On November 16, 2010, after eight years of dating, the happy couple made the official announcement that a royal wedding was soon to come.

At Home with the Cambridges

The London weather forecast for April 29, 2011, called for cold northeasterly winds, drizzling rain, and a possible thunderstorm, but that made little difference to a million spectators lining the streets of London that morning. Gathered beneath dozens of red, blue, and white British flags strung overhead, the crowd hoped for a glimpse of the world's most famous

A million spectators line the streets of London to watch William and Kate travel from Westminster Abbey to Buckingham Palace on their wedding day. Two billion people watched the wedding broadcast on TV worldwide.

The Bride with No Title

A wedding like that of Prince William and Catherine Middleton in 2011 had not happened in 351 years. That was the last time a future king of England had married a commoner, someone with no royal rank or title. In 1660, the Duke of York (who later became King James II) married Anne Hyde, a maid to the princess of the Netherlands. To delay the unavoidable public scorn, their wedding took place at midnight and was kept a secret for months.

Centuries later, William proudly married Catherine in broad daylight before a large crowd, ignoring snide comments from some aristocrats about Catherine's working-class ancestors, some of whom had been coal miners and builders. It seemed times had changed, and most British citizens were willing to accept a commoner as their future queen.

In 2012, Australian students researching Catherine's genealogy for a class project discovered that the new Duchess of Cambridge actually did have a royal branch in her family tree. She was distantly related to earls, countesses, and even a prime minister. In fact, she and William have a common ancestor and are distant cousins. Still, Catherine will likely go down in history as the commoner who became a queen.

bride. When Kate and her father stepped out of a black 1977 Rolls-Royce in front of Westminster Abbey, the street erupted in cheers. Kate's sister, Pippa, fluffed the elegant wedding gown's long train before England's most famous commoner disappeared inside the thousand-year-old church to marry the prince who waited at the altar in full military uniform.

Nineteen hundred guests attended the two-hour ceremony. When it was over, Kate and William stepped into an open-top carriage for a ride through the crowd-lined streets of London to Buckingham Palace. There, standing with their families on the balcony overlooking the tree-lined road known as the Mall, the royal couple shared their first married kiss in front of a sea of cheering onlookers. As royal jets flew by overhead, William and Kate delighted the crowd by kissing again before heading off to a series of private receptions that lasted well into the early morning hours.

The event was the happy ending to a Cinderella-like love story that had captivated the world. In addition to the million-strong crowd on the streets of London, 2 billion people around the globe watched live coverage of the long-awaited royal wedding. Will and Kate had become the most famous bride and groom in history.

Life After the Wedding

British custom dictates that royal grooms and brides are given new titles on their wedding day. William already had the title Prince William of Wales, but in honor of his marriage, Queen Elizabeth also dubbed him the Duke of Cambridge, the Earl of Strathearn (of Scotland), and Baron Carrickfergus (of Ireland), giving him royal ties throughout the British Isles. The former Catherine Middleton was now the Duchess of Cambridge, Countess of Strathearn, Baroness Carrickfergus, and Princess William of Wales. She is not officially called Princess Kate or Princess Catherine, because she is part of the royal family by marriage and therefore takes her husband's name.

Despite their new regal titles, William and Kate were still two generations away from the throne. The queen was eighty-five years old when they married, but she was still very active and respected in her role as the British monarch, and Charles and Camilla had long been next in line to take over royal duties. William and Kate were tremendously popular around the world, with as much as 62 percent of British people reporting in various polls that they would like to see William become the next king, but the young royals had years to wait and things they wanted to do in the meantime. "I think he has now found his royal life rather boring and feels he is worth more than just shaking hands,"[34] an anonymous friend of the couple is quoted as saying of William.

A Dress to Remember

No detail of William and Kate's wedding created more stir than the bride's dress. In one of the best-kept fashion secrets of all time, the fabled gown remained a complete surprise for all but a handful of people until the moment the bride stepped out of a car in front of Westminster Abbey for her wedding.

Kate chose long, lacy sleeves, a full skirt, and a nine-foot train to resemble the dress American actress Grace Kelly wore when she married the prince of Monaco in 1956. (Like Kate, Grace Kelly was a commoner.) Sheets of handmade lace in the shape of roses, thistles, daffodils, and shamrocks adorned Kate's satin skirt and bodice. The back of the dress had fifty-eight tiny buttons, each covered in fabric and fastened with a loop.

Those who helped make the dress had to wash their hands every thirty minutes to keep the fabric pristine, although none of them knew who would be wearing their creation. The dress's designer, Sarah Burton, was strictly forbidden to tell anyone she was designing the world's most famous bridal gown. Defying even the most determined reporters, Kate managed to keep her dress veiled in secrecy until her wedding day.

The formality of their new status did little to change their casual approach to life. Immediately after the wedding weekend, William returned to work as a search-and-rescue helicopter pilot, postponing his and Kate's honeymoon until May when he had two weeks of leave from his job. William knew he and Kate would have to spend a certain amount of time attending public engagements, but he wanted to devote a few years of his life to his dream career of helping people in distress. At heart, William saw himself as a military man. "It has been a real privilege to have spent the past year understanding and experiencing all aspects of the British Armed Forces," he had said in 2010. "I now want to build on the experience and training I have received. . . . Joining Search and Rescue is the perfect opportunity for me to serve in the Forces operationally."[35]

The Duke and Duchess at Home

After their wedding, William and Kate could have chosen to live in a palace or castle, but they instead rented a rustic four-bedroom farmhouse on the Isle of Anglesey off the coast of Wales, where William was stationed with the Royal Air Force. The queen had granted the newlyweds two years of freedom to live as they wished without a demanding schedule of royal appearances, and in their private Anglesey home, which they shared with just one housekeeper, they were content to shun the fussiness of royal life. Kate often was seen pushing her own shopping cart through aisles of the local supermarket or carrying a bag of groceries home. "The Duchess dressed casually and never wore make-up," says Michael Thornton, a royal biographer who lives in Anglesey. "The people here are not terribly royalist-minded and were ambivalent, at best, about their arrival, but she and William won Anglesey over with their warmth and low-key lifestyle."[36]

William and Kate acted and were treated no differently than the rest of the townspeople. They liked to go for jogs on the farmhouse's private beach, and occasionally they rode William's motorcycle to a local restaurant or pub, but mostly they stayed home by the fireplace. Kate liked to have dinner waiting for William when he came home from work, especially his favorite dish, roast chicken. On weekends and evenings they were fans of staying indoors and watching movies and television series on DVD with their cocker spaniel puppy, Lupo. "It's all very normal," an anonymous friend of the couple told *Vanity Fair* magazine. "The last time I went round, William was pottering around making tea and toast, very chilled and relaxed."[37]

William's devotion to his career and Kate's down-to-earth commonness made the couple popular with the public. For the

While William was stationed with the Royal Air Force as a search and rescue pilot, he and Kate led a quiet life in the remote town of Anglesey, Wales.

first time anyone could recall, there were members of the British monarchy who were relatable and lived much as any average young couple might. That was exactly what William and Kate wanted.

Queenly Kate

Although Kate was undeniably comfortable with everyday things, when the occasion called for a more stately presence, little was common about the new Duchess of Cambridge. She blended seamlessly into the challenging social rituals of royal public life, attending royal events and occasions with William and always looking both elegant and kind. In private, she had undergone etiquette training to master all the tiny but crucial rituals of royal society, everything from curtsying and holding silverware to the proper way to get in and out of a car, but she quickly mastered

As part of her royal duties Kate takes part in a day of activities and festivities—including a game of field hockey—at St. Andrews School in 2012.

princess protocol and avoided embarrassing breaches of dignity. Despite the formality required of a royal, Kate also brought a person-centered approach to her public appearances, much like Princess Diana had always done. She looked people in the eye and greeted them warmly when shaking hands, and she would crouch down when needed to place herself on eye level with people. In the fall of 2012, Kate visited her former boarding school, St. Andrews, and delighted the students by participating in a game of field hockey in a dress and high-heeled boots. "It's rather surreal knowing that she will be Queen one day, but by all accounts she is as refreshingly normal as always,"[38] one of her former classmates commented after the event.

Kate brought humility, grace, and fun to the royal family. Both at home and at fancy royal engagements, she was comfortable with her role as a prince's wife. "(William) chose very well," says Richard Palmer, a royal correspondent for the British press. "She is perfect princess material. She is very elegant, and very stable. They both seem good for one another."[39]

Royal Scandals

Life for the new duke and duchess was not always as private, peaceful, and down to earth as they perhaps would have liked. Kate's classic, accessible, and affordable style had made her one of the most photographed women in the world. The young couple was plagued by the ever-present paparazzi that had always been a source of stress for William.

In September 2012, an invasion of royal privacy erupted in scandal. During a private vacation at the Château d'Autet in the South of France, the normally demure Kate took off her bathing suit top, not knowing she was in view of a cameraman's telephoto lens about half a mile (1km) away. To the humiliation of the entire royal family, photographs of the topless duchess were published in the French edition of the British tabloid *Closer* and circulated around the world on tabloid covers and the Internet.

The issue spawned a great deal of controversy. Some conservatives raised disapproving eyebrows at the duchess's immodest approach to sunbathing. Many people, however, countered that a young married couple was entitled to privacy and should not have been hounded by the press when they clearly believed they were alone. Much of the scorn for the scandal was directed at *Closer*. "The incident is reminiscent of the worst excesses of the press and paparazzi during the life of Diana, Princess of Wales, and all the more upsetting to the duke and duchess for being so," said a statement issued from St. James's Palace, the royal office of William and Kate. "Their Royal Highnesses had every expectation of privacy in the remote house. It is unthinkable that anyone should take such photographs, let alone publish them."[40]

The duke and duchess's security team also received sharp criticism for failing to notice the paparazzo. "If a photographer can poke a lens through some greenery and take these type of pictures then a gunman with a high-powered weapon and telescopic sight could have done far worse," says Ken Wharfe, a former guard of Princess Diana. "How this area was not checked out by their security people is unbelievable. These shots were taken from a public road,"[41] Wharfe fumed. Fifteen years after French paparazzi were believed to have had a role in the death of William's mother, the incident revived emotional issues of the royal family's safety and privacy in an increasingly media-centered world.

A Mysterious Illness

In the months that followed, the scandal of the topless photos was overshadowed by persistent rumors that Kate might be pregnant. People analyzed every photo of the duchess to see whether her waistline was a bit rounder or whether she seemed to be holding her purse in front of her in public. On December 3, 2012, the public was alarmed when Kate was admitted to London's King Edward VII Hospital. To dispel potential rumors about the nature of her illness, the palace was forced to make a formal announcement: "Their Royal Highnesses the Duke and Duchess of Cambridge are very pleased to announce that the Duchess of Cambridge is expecting a baby."[42] Newspapers revealed that Kate was suffering from severe morning sickness and had been hospitalized to restore fluids and nutrients.

William and Kate leave the King Edward VII hospital in London, England, on December 6, 2012, four days after she was admitted for treatment for acute morning sickness.

The formal announcement that a new royal baby was on the way only increased the press's enthusiastic pursuit of the royal couple. On the morning of December 4, 2012, two Australian radio hosts called the hospital and pretended to be Queen Elizabeth and Prince Charles seeking news about Kate's status. The nurse who took the phone call, Jacintha Saldanha, fell for the impersonation and put the call through to another nurse, who revealed confidential information about the duchess's condition. The radio station played the recorded phone conversation and put the sound clips up on its website. Once again, the press was harshly criticized for a brazen intrusion into Kate and William's private lives. "Our nurses are caring, professional people trained to look after patients, not to cope with journalistic trickery of this sort,"[43] the hospital's chief executive, John Lofthouse, told reporters.

The incident was meant as a joke, but three days later, Saldanha was found dead after an apparent suicide. She had left a note implying that the radio hoax had a role in her death. The tragic incident highlighted once again the stressful and potentially devastating effects of the constant media attention that surrounds every aspect of royal life.

Welcoming a New Prince into the World

Aside from the severe morning sickness that put her in the hospital and led to the radio hoax, Kate's pregnancy was generally a time of joy for the royal family and its fans. Around the world, other women who were expecting babies looked to the trend-setting duchess for guidance on maternity clothing styles, and almost anything similar to what Kate was seen wearing in the spring of 2013 quickly became a sellout item. Kate especially favored clothing from a London store called Seraphine for her maternity fashions, and other pregnant women soon did as well. According to Seraphine designer Cecile Reinaud, "In two days we did the turnover that we would do in a month. It's kind of a game changer, in terms of the appeal that she has."[44]

During the summer, the news that the duchess was in labor hit headlines worldwide. Prince George Alexander Louis of Cambridge was born July 22, 2013, at St. Mary's Hospital in London—the same hospital where William had arrived thirty-one years earlier. Crowds clamored outside the hospital the next day when a normally private Will and Kate emerged with the new prince, whose birth had put him ahead of his uncle Harry in line to one day take the British throne. "I was on such a high anyway, and so was Catherine, about George that really we were

Kate and William leave St. Mary's Hospital with Prince George on July 23, 2013. Even with the media circus outside the hospital, William insisted on carrying on as normally as possible, installing the infant car seat himself and driving his wife and new baby home.

happy to show him off to whoever wanted to see him,"[45] William recalls.

Despite the fanfare and excitement over the newest heir to the throne, William quickly went back to his desire to be normal, even in royal fatherhood. When it was time to take the baby prince home, the duke insisted on installing the infant car seat himself and being the one behind the wheel. "I am as indepen-

An Heir in Blue—or Pink

When the Duchess of Cambridge went into labor in July 2013, the event was especially historic. For the first time in centuries, the soon-to-arrive royal baby had a guaranteed throne waiting in his—or *her*—future.

The British royal order of succession is the sequence in which members of the royal family are in line to take the throne. The order, established in 1701, laid out specific rules about who could become the next king or queen. A royal son always edged out older sisters, if he had any, in a process called male primogeniture. (Queen Elizabeth II became queen in 1952 only because she had no brothers.) In April 2013, the British Parliament changed the law, stating that the firstborn child of a reigning monarch's firstborn child would be next in line for the throne—regardless of the child's sex. Prince George was therefore unique in being the first British baby guaranteed a straight path to the throne, even if he had been born a girl.

dent as I want to be, same as Catherine," he says. "I very much feel if that I can do it myself, I want to do it myself. . . . I think driving your son and your wife away from hospital was really important to me."[46]

Moving to the Palace

The addition of George was the first of many coming changes to William and Kate's quiet, private life on the Welsh island. In August 2013, just weeks after the birth of his son, William announced his retirement from the Royal Air Force. He, his father, and his grandmother all felt it was time for William to have a more visible public role in royal affairs, tours, and appearances. The busy schedule would leave less time for a full-time job as

After he retired from the Royal Air Force, William and Kate moved into a twenty-two room apartment in Kensington Palace.

a pilot, quiet beachside walks, and home-cooked dinners with Kate and their new baby. It would also require the couple to move to London, where they would be closer to the rest of the royal family and more accessible to the public.

In September 2013, William, Kate, and George moved to a four-story apartment in Kensington Palace, next door to where William and Harry had spent much of their childhood with Diana. For Kate, who had felt very at home in the rustic setting of the Anglesey farmhouse, the lifestyle change was drastic. A million-dollar renovation of the twenty-two rooms in her and William's new home included such upgrades as his-and-hers bathrooms, a daytime and a nighttime nursery for George, a basement coffee room for their household staff, and a family kitchen so Kate could still prepare some meals. With a full cleaning and cooking staff at her disposal, however, Kate no longer went shopping for groceries.

Privacy once again became a rarity for the couple, with photographers camped outside of the palace for any glimpse of royals. The experience, at times, could be daunting. "It's nerve-racking because I don't know the ropes really,"[47] Kate said about adjusting to the pressures of the royal lifestyle. At Kensington Palace, there were a lot of ropes to learn.

A King in Training

William, meanwhile, found himself in the rapidly expanding role of being second in line to the throne. The queen, at age eighty-seven, was one of the longest-serving British monarchs in history and had headed the royal family for as long as almost anyone alive could remember, but she was slowing down. Occasional health problems began to interfere with her royal appearances, and travel was becoming more difficult for her with every passing year. She had begun to share responsibilities with Charles and Camilla, both in their mid-sixties, but William and Kate were also taking on larger roles. Britain's younger population found they could identify with the new royal parents who liked to do things themselves. William and Kate brought a sense of youth and excitement to the aging monarchy, and they were finally in a position to put their fame to work.

Philanthropy and Royal Duties

On Sunday, June 3, 2012, a thousand boats from Great Britain and around the world converged on the River Thames that runs through London. Queen Elizabeth II sat on a barge in the center of the parade, which was a central event of the four-day weekend celebrating her sixtieth year as queen.

Not since 1897 had people seen a celebration quite like it. That was the year of Queen Victoria's Diamond Jubilee and the first time the term had been used to describe a celebration of six decades on the throne. Victoria, Elizabeth's great-great-grandmother, is the only other British monarch in history to rule for sixty years. Elizabeth's own Jubilee celebrated the tremendous growth of the Commonwealth of Nations, a voluntary organization of independent countries headed by the reigning British monarch, which had grown from seven nations at the time of Elizabeth's coronation in 1952 to fifty-four by her Diamond Jubilee. Every Commonwealth nation hoped for a visit from the royal family that year. William and Kate joined Charles and Camilla, William's uncles, and even Prince Harry in dividing up the overwhelming schedule of visits and appearances around the globe.

On William and Kate's agenda were visits to the Southeast Asian nations of Malaysia and Singapore and the Pacific Island nations of the Solomon Islands and Tuvalu in September 2012. The nine-day visit was the young couple's second royal tour together as representatives of the British monarchy, their

Heroically Royal

Intense winds struck the Irish Sea in the middle of the night on November 27, 2011. Around 2 A.M., a mayday call came in to the Royal Air Force's helicopter base on the Welsh island of Anglesey. A cargo ship with eight crew members had sunk in the icy water. A British rescue helicopter took off immediately and navigated the storm to rescue two of the ship's crew members. Copiloting the helicopter was Flight Lieutenant William Wales, better known to most of his countrymen as Prince William.

During his years of service with the Royal Air Force, William undertook 156 search-and-rescue operations that saved 149 people, often in dangerously stormy conditions. The people he helped to pluck from raging ocean waters or frozen mountaintops did not always realize that the heir to the throne was risking his own life to fly them to safety.

William may one day wear the royal crown, but he found his true passion while dressed in a helicopter pilot's flight uniform and helmet.

first having come fourteen months earlier when they had visited Canada and the United States. With as many as eight or nine public events scheduled every day, the Pacific Islands visit was a whirlwind sampling of the often hectic and enormously public world of royal duty that was destined to become the young couple's future.

Olympic Madness

The summer of 2012 marked another major event in Britain that demanded a royal presence from Will and Kate, but this one was closer to home. The two joined Prince Harry as ambassadors for the 2012 Summer Olympics in London. It was a role usually reserved for former Olympians, but given the royals' youth

Kate and William and other fans rejoice as the British team wins gold and sets a new world record in men's sprint track cycling during the 2012 Olympic Games in London, England.

and natural athleticism, representing the monarchy at the games was a perfect fit. In the months leading up to the Olympics, the three joined twenty-seven other ambassadors as they visited British teams and athletes. During the games themselves, Kate especially shined in her first national role as a royal. "Her support has meant so much," Olympic hockey player Alex Danson told reporters. "To have Kate here makes me feel so proud to be British."[48]

William and Kate's Olympic schedule started with their attending the opening ceremonies on July 27 and continued nonstop for the next two weeks as they supported nine hundred British athletes and attended parties and other occasions. Their Olympic duties were not all ceremonial. There was time to watch their favorite events—hockey and sailing for Kate, tennis and football (or soccer, in the United States) for William. Kate also found time in the months leading up to the games to practice with the field hockey team, where she showed them what a duchess was made of. “I was determined to keep on going until I scored,”[49] the athletic Kate said after scoring a goal. During the games, she and William were also caught by the “kiss cam,” the crowd-scanning camera seeking smooching fans, as they shared a quick embrace.

Baby on Board

William and Kate’s popularity was only magnified when Prince George arrived a year later. The royal couple was now a royal family, and Kate and William were quickly upstaged by their

William, Kate, and George look at a bilby—named George in honor of the young prince—during a visit to Sydney’s Taronga Zoo in 2014.

chubby-cheeked baby. Decades earlier, Princess Diana had shocked royal traditionalists by taking her sons with her and Charles when they went on royal tours. William and Kate readily followed suit with their own child. Just as a nine-month-old William had visited Australia and New Zealand, so, too, did nine-month-old George in spring 2014. He even attended a gathering with ten other babies where the duke and duchess, always candid about parenthood, swapped stories with other parents.

Ever concerned about limiting the strain of public engagements for his wife and baby, William kept George's public appearances to a minimum in Australia just as he did back home in London. "William knows only too well that his baby son will be the new favorite creature in the circus he grew up in," says newspaper columnist Allison Pearson. "Every plan he and Kate have put in place is to protect him."[50] Still, George tremendously boosted public excitement wherever the duke and duchess took him.

The Serious Side of Being Royal

Despite the smiles and family affection that shined through in photographs of the young royal family on their Australian visit, William and Kate had chosen to go there in part because of a tragedy that had occurred on February 22, 2011. Christchurch, New Zealand's oldest and second-largest city, was devastated by a powerful earthquake that had killed 185 people and injured thousands. The tremors destroyed more than half the buildings in the city's business district. Damaged water supplies and sewage systems made the city completely uninhabitable. That same winter, the Australian states of Victoria and Queensland were damaged by severe floods.

In 2011, William had visited the disaster sites in New Zealand and Australia. During his return in 2014, he again met with victims, this time with Kate at his side. The royal couple showed that caring, compassion, and public service would be mainstays of their royal duties. "We look up to royalty and to have the future King of England come here and recognise us for some of the things we did is quite gratifying,"[51] says Terry Gyde, one of the Christchurch firemen who spoke with William.

Survivors of New Zealand's worst natural disaster were not the only victims the duke and duchess tried to cheer during their spring 2014 trip. Among other engagements, they visited the Bear Cottage Hospice, a care center for children with terminal illnesses. They spent time with a baby, about the same age as Prince George, who was dying of bacterial meningitis. The couple stayed so long to meet and talk to families that they delayed the rest of the day's schedule. Before she left, Kate told staff members, "It's very inspiring but we're also ready for a big sob."[52] Children's hospice services have since become a cause the duke and duchess strongly support.

Royal Charity

Charitable service is one of the most important responsibilities of the royal family, and William and Kate use their celebrity status to bring attention to causes that are important to them.

Altogether, the royal family supports about three thousand charitable organizations around the world, but each member of the family has favorites. William, and since 2011, Kate, have chosen causes they are passionate about, both as a couple and as individuals. The publicity and fund-raising power they bring to social issues is one of the privileges of being part of the royal family.

Philanthropy is nothing new to either William or Kate, both of whom volunteered to help with environmental causes and to assist disadvantaged children in Chile before they even met each other at the University of St. Andrews. William, especially, was raised to seek involvement in charity work. His mother was known around Britain and the world for her tireless work to help people who were homeless, sick, injured, or disabled. William has carried on his mother's legacy of helping others by championing such causes as military veterans, disadvantaged children, and environmental conservation.

Two particular places where the duke spends time are organizations that were also dear to Diana—Centrepoint, a charity for homeless children and teens in London, and London-based Royal Marsden Hospital, the largest cancer-care center in Europe. William made secret visits to Centrepoint with his mother when he was a child, and in 2005 he spent a freezing winter night outdoors to bring public attention to the struggles of the homeless. That same year, William chose Centrepoint as the first organization to which he would become a patron by lending his name as its official royal supporter, thus becoming a

Prince William visits Christchurch Cathedral in March 2011. The church suffered significant damage during an earthquake a month earlier.

world-recognized spokesperson to draw attention to the cause and encourage people to support it by making donations.

In 2007, William also became a patron of the Royal Marsden Hospital, where he is known for sitting down to talk with cancer patients and serving them tea. "When he first came here, he spent quite a lot of time with the patients on our breast cancer ward and the next day, he sent everybody he met a bouquet with a handwritten note," says Cally Palmer, the hospital's chief executive. "He has fantastic empathy with patients. . . . They feel inspired by him when he's here."[53] Palmer and Seyi Obakin,

Kate visits The Brink, an alcohol-free bar for people recovering from alcohol and drug addiction in Liverpool, England, in 2012. The woman at the blender is making a smoothie called the Duchess.

chief executive of Centrepoint, both received invitations to William and Kate's wedding in 2011, as did one of Centrepoint's formerly homeless teens who had become particularly special to the prince.

Kate, too, quickly made public service a large part of her royal role. Since officially becoming the Duchess of Cambridge, she has championed many causes, including art and natural history museums. Like Diana, Kate also especially favors charities that help children. She is passionate about helping hospices that provide care for children with terminal illnesses, and she is a patron of a program that provides school-based mental and emotional support to children facing difficult social issues. As a patron of Action on Addiction, she supports programs that help to free people from substance abuse and to aid the children of those struggling with addiction. Kate also supports a charity that uses art therapy to reach out to unhappy children, and she is a patron of SportsAid, an organization that helps young athletes achieve their dreams.

Kate also is known to change out of a designer dress into blue jeans and a Girl Scouts scarf when the situation calls for it. A former scout herself, she was a frequent volunteer with local scout troops when she and William lived in Anglesey after they got married. In November 2013, a smiling Kate braved freezing temperatures and blizzard conditions as she volunteered to help young girls learn to build campfires and make bread. "The Duchess has an incredibly busy life, which makes it all the more inspiring that she has chosen to volunteer alongside us,"[54] says reality TV star and chief scout Bear Grylls. Kate combines her famous royal image with her down-to-earth side to benefit people and causes that are close to her heart.

The Royal Foundation

Both William and Kate put a personal touch on their volunteer efforts by taking time to sit down and talk with people from all walks of life, but they also use their fame to raise money for their favorite causes. In 2009, Princes William and Harry started their own foundation, an organization that collects money to donate to charitable causes. When William and Kate got married, the princes added the duchess to what is now called the Royal Foundation of the Duke and Duchess of Cambridge and Prince Harry. "For reasons that never cease to amaze us, we do seem to be able to bring a spotlight to bear on wonderful initiatives created by other people to help those in need,"[55] say William, Harry, and Kate on the foundation's website.

The Royal Foundation supports three main causes: the armed forces, young people, and conservation. Among the causes that have received Royal Foundation funding are endangered species, secondary-school programs in Uganda, and the victims of the Christchurch earthquake in New Zealand. The Invictus Games, a sporting event for wounded, injured, and ill members of the British armed forces, is also one of the Royal Foundation's partners. In the United States, the duke and duchess have held fund-raising activities for the American Friends of The Foundation of Prince William and Prince Harry, a partner organization that focuses on U.S. veterans, children, and environmental conservation.

Harry, William, and Kate interact with students at Bacon's College in London, England, while launching their foundation's Coach Core program, in 2012.

Funding for the foundation's various programs comes from many sources. When William and Kate got married, they requested that wedding guests and well-wishers donate to their foundation through the Wedding Charity Fund instead of buying gifts. The Wedding Charity Fund collected more than £1 million ($1.7 million), a sum that was divided among six different charities.

William and Kate have been active in organizing high-profile events and donating the proceeds to their foundation and other charities. On November 26, 2013, they hosted a concert at Kensington Palace featuring singers Jon Bon Jovi and Taylor Swift. The event raised £1 million ($1.7 million) for Centrepoint and also became an Internet sensation when video footage of William jumping on stage to sing with Bon Jovi and Swift went viral. "We came to join forces if you will, and throw a little international light on our foundation,"[56] says Bon Jovi, who individually also raises money for people who are homeless or living in poverty.

Back to Home-Cooked Meals

As famous public figures, representatives of the royal family worldwide, and active volunteers for a wide variety of charities, William and Kate lead very busy lives. Nevertheless, they still long for the normalcy of life as average citizens. In summer 2014, less than a year after he and Kate moved with George into Kensington Palace in London, William announced that he had taken a job in the private sector as a helicopter pilot with a company called East Anglia Air Ambulance. "I don't think there's any greater calling in life,"[57] he said about his passion for helicopter rescue missions.

The change would force William to return to a schedule of only part-time royal duties, as he would be very busy with his new full-time job. This was a bold and unexpected choice for the prince, who became the first heir to the throne to ever accept a paying civilian job. After a six-month training program, William was expected to commit at least two years to his job as an air ambulance helicopter pilot. The job paid a yearly salary of

Taylor Swift, Jon Bon Jovi, and Prince William (left to right), perform at a London, England, charity gala in November 2013. The event raised $1.7 million and a video of the performance went viral.

£40,000 ($66,000), out of which William paid taxes—another first for an heir to the throne—before donating the remainder to charity. He and Kate also announced they were moving away from London and taking George to live on the royal family's Sandringham House in eastern England in order to be close to William's job. Not long after that decision, the royal family made still another announcement in September 2014—Kate was pregnant again.

Despite the news of a second royal baby on the way, not everyone was pleased with the prince's tradition-breaking decision to return to a more civilian—and family based—life. Many people felt William was shirking his responsibility to help the aging queen with her royal duties. It was clear, however, that William was determined not to let royal demands overpower his and Kate's own plans for their lives. "He is his own man," says royal commentator Robert Jobson. "He is considering options other than becoming a full-time royal devoted to engagements that his birthright demands. . . . William wants to preside over a more modern monarchy and this is his chance to shape it."[58] The royal couple welcomed a daughter, Princess Charlotte Elizabeth Diana, May 2, 2015.

A Monarchy for the Future

William and Kate's balance between being royalty and just an everyday husband and wife is unusual, but it may be just what the monarchy needs. For decades, there have been people throughout Great Britain and the Commonwealth of Nations

Princess Charlotte Elizabeth Diana was born at St. Mary's Hospital in London, like her father and big brother George. William and Kate welcomed their second child on May 2, 2015.

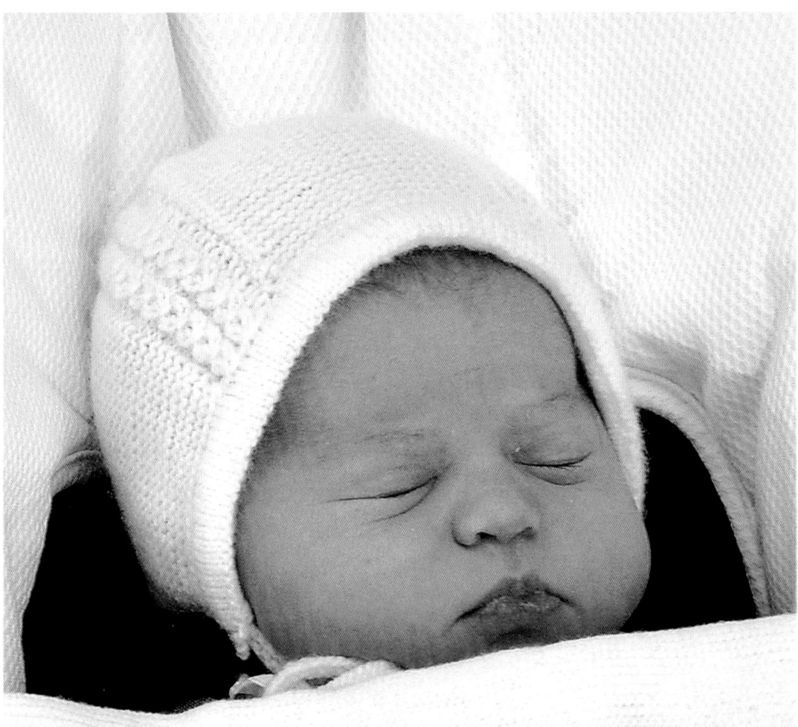

Raising Royalty

Princess Diana broke with tradition in many ways, but no more so than in her parenting choices. When it came time to welcome their own children into the world, William and Kate followed Diana's trend of *not* following royal trends. Kate became the first member of the royal family to have a baby shower. As Diana had done, Kate gave birth in a hospital instead of at Buckingham Palace, even choosing the same hospital where William had been born. The Cambridges dodged another royal custom when they spent the first weeks of George's life at the home of Kate's parents rather than at a palace. Kate's mother served as the prince's earliest nanny, and her father took on the role of royal photographer, since Kate and William wanted no one except for security guards intruding on their new family.

Baby George, unlike his royal predecessors, had no full-time nanny. His mom and dad wanted to experience hands-on parenting. William even changed George's first diaper. At royal appearances after becoming parents, Kate was often seen with baby George on her hip.

who have questioned the need for a monarchy in modern times. Lawmaking and most other government tasks are carried out by elected members of Parliament, Britain's governing body, and the prime minister, but the monarch has an important role as an adviser to Parliament and all new bills must have royal consent. Some people in Britain and other Commonwealth nations want to abolish the monarchy and see Britain become a pure republic, a nation where the people are fully led by elected representatives and there is no longer a king or queen. "In a democratic society there is no room for a head of state who is put there for life and by birth,"[59] says Graham Smith, chief executive of an organization called Republic that campaigns against keeping the monarchy.

When polled, a majority of British and Commonwealth citizens consistently say they admire the royal family and feel that the monarchy is necessary. Just the same, many people say they resent their tax dollars' being spent on lavish royal lifestyles and events like William and Kate's wedding, for which security cost British taxpayers about £20 million ($33 million), or Queen Elizabeth's yearlong Diamond Jubilee, during which the public cost of supporting the royal family rose by about £1 million ($1.7 million). Prince William and Prince Harry themselves contributed to much controversy in their teens and early twenties. They were often photographed drinking at expensive nightclubs, which led to their being criticized as spoiled members of the privileged class with little understanding of or connection to the lives of regular people.

William's choice in 2014 to put a career and his growing family ahead of royal duty, along with his and Kate's preference for an unpretentious lifestyle, have done much to improve public opinion of royalty and make the monarchy seem both approachable and in touch with everyday citizens. It sometimes seems the Duke and Duchess of Cambridge lead double lives, switching between the publicized glitz of royal events and the comforts of a backyard barbecue or a roast chicken dinner by the fireplace. As long as they are still two generations away from the throne, however, Will and Kate seem content to live as commonly as possible while waiting for royal duty to call. The couple's rare mix of glamour and humility has been met with curiosity and admiration from people around the world.

Introduction

1. Quoted in Lauren Effron and Luchina Fisher. "William and Kate Take L.A.: What Is It About the Royal Couple That Fascinates Even Hollywood?" ABC News, July 8, 2011. http://abcnews.go.com/Entertainment/Kate-middleton-prince-williams-celebrity-status/story?id=14030146.

Chapter 1: William the Wombat

2. Joann F. Price. *Prince William: A Biography*. Santa Barbara, CA: Greenwood, 2011, pp. 17–18.
3. Quoted in ABC News. "Princess Diana's Legacy of Motherhood for Kate." ABC News blogs, July 1, 2013. https://gma.yahoo.com/blogs/abc-news-blogs/princess-dianas-legacy-motherhood-kate-143403880.html.
4. Quoted in Tim Graham and Peter Archer. *William: HRH Prince William of Wales*. New York: Atria, 2003, p. 52.
5. Quoted in Katie Nicholl. *William and Harry: Behind the Palace Walls*. New York: Weinstein Books, 2010, p. 28.
6. Quoted in Rob Wallace. "'Rebel Royal Mum': Diana's Legacy as Parent." ABC News, May 26, 2013. http://abcnews.go.com/International/rebel-royal-mum-dianas-legacy-parent/story?id=19241646.
7. Quoted in Nicholl. *William and Harry*, p. 68.
8. Quoted in Bill Glauber. "William Comes to Adulthood Cautiously." *Baltimore Sun*, June 17, 2000. http://articles.baltimoresun.com/2000-06-17/features/0006170104_1_prince-william-royal-monarchy.
9. Quoted in *The Telegraph* (London). "Prince William Hid Grief over Diana's Death to 'Protect Himself,'" May 7, 2012. www.telegraph.co.uk/news/uknews/prince-william/9250118/Prince-William-hid-grief-over-Dianas-death-to-protect-himself.html.
10. Quoted in Matt Lauer. "In Honor of Diana: Two Princes Speak on the 10th Anniversary of Their Mother's Death."

Transcript. *Dateline NBC*, June 19, 2007. www.nbcnews.com/id/19190534/ns/dateline_nbc-.

11. Quoted in BBC News. "2000: Prince William's Expedition to Chile." Video. March 22, 2011. www.bbc.co.uk/news/uk-12509014.

Chapter 2: Kate the Commoner

12. Quoted in *MailOnline*. "How Kate Told Friends About Her 'Perfect, Natural' Labour and Kept Her Hairdresser on Call for a Whole Month Before Prince George's Birth," September 5, 2013. www.dailymail.co.uk/femail/article-2413052/Kate-Middleton-told-friends-baby-Prince-Georges-perfect-natural-labour.html.
13. Quoted in Eman el-Shenawi. "Kate Middleton Had Happy Times as a Child in Jordan." Al Arabiya News, April 28, 2011. http://english.alarabiya.net/articles/2011/04/28/147138.html.
14. Quoted in Sean Smith. *Kate: A Biography of Kate Middleton*. London: Simon & Schuster, 2011. E-book edition.
15. Quoted in Katie Nicholl. *Kate: The Future Queen*. New York: Weinstein, 2013. E-book edition.
16. Quoted in Fay Schlesinger and Hannah Roberts. "Kate Was Bullied at Her £30,000 'Insidious' Girls' School 'for Being Too Skinny and Meek.'" *MailOnline*, April 3, 2011. www.dailymail.co.uk/femail/article-1373036/Kate-Middleton-bullied-30k-girls-school-skinny-meek.html#ixzz390KvOtD7.
17. Quoted in Celia Denison. "The Mother of the Year." *Tatler*, May 8, 2013. www.tatler.com/news/articles/may-2013/mother-of-the-year---carole-middleton.
18. Quoted in Stephen Bates. "How 'Commoner' Kate Middleton Won Prince William's Heart." *Guardian* (Manchester, UK), November 16, 2010. www.theguardian.com/uk/2010/nov/17/kate-middleton-prince-william-engagement.
19. Quoted in *Telegraph* (London). "Royal Wedding: Prince William and Kate Middleton Interview in Full," November 17, 2010. www.telegraph.co.uk/news/uknews/royal

-wedding/8138904/Royal-Wedding-Prince-William-and-Kate-Middleton-interview-in-full.html.
20. Quoted in Ross Lydall. "Revealed . . . How Kate Followed William on His Chile Mission." *London Evening Standard*, April 21, 2011. www.standard.co.uk/news/revealed-how-kate-followed-william-on-his-chile-mission-6394962.html.

Chapter 3: Will and Kate

21. Quoted in Katie Nicholl. "Kate: The Making of a Very Middle Class Princess (Part 1)." *MailOnline*, November 20, 2010. www.dailymail.co.uk/femail/article-1331545/Kate-Middleton-The-making-middle-class-Princess-PART-1.html.
22. Quoted in Susannah Palk. "College Friend Reveals Kate and William's Early Romance." CNN World, April 20, 2011. www.cnn.com/2011/WORLD/europe/04/20/uk.william.kate.university.
23. Quoted in Christopher P. Andersen. *William and Kate: A Royal Love Story*. New York: Gallery, 2011, p. 124.
24. Quoted in *MailOnline*. "Is This the New People's Princess? How Confident Kate Middleton Compares to 'Shy Di,'" November 17, 2010. www.dailymail.co.uk/femail/article-1330165/Royal-engagement-How-Kate-Middleton-compares-Shy-Di.html.
25. Andersen. *William and Kate*, p. 127.
26. Quoted in Sarah Price Brown. "Britain's Royal Family Attends Prince William's University Graduation." *Baltimore Sun*, June 24, 2005. http://articles.baltimoresun.com/2005-06-24/news/0506240286_1_prince-william-prince-charles-graduation.
27. Quoted in *Telegraph*. "Royal Wedding."
28. Quoted in *Telegraph*. "Royal Wedding."
29. Emma Garman. "How Kate Became a Princess." *The Awl*, February 15, 2012. www.theawl.com/2012/02/how-kate-became-a-princess.
30. Quoted in *MailOnline*. "I'm Too Young to Marry, Says William," April 1, 2005. www.dailymail.co.uk/news/article

-343317/Im-young-marry-says-William.html.

31. Quoted in Marcia Moody. "Secrets of the Royal Romantic Reunion That Changed the Course of History: What Really Made Kate and Wills Rekindle Their Love—and Transform the Monarchy Forever." *MailOnline*, July 8, 2013. www.dailymail.co.uk/femail/article-2357494/What-really-Kate-Middleton-Prince-William-rekindle-love--secrets-romantic-reunion-.html.
32. Quoted in Svenja O'Donnell. "William Waited to Propose to Let Kate 'Back Out' of Joining Royal Family." Bloomberg, November 16, 2010. www.bloomberg.com/news/2010-11-17/william-waited-to-propose-to-let-kate-back-out-of-joining-royal-family.html.
33. Quoted in *MailOnline*. "Pictured: The Remote Kenyan Hut Where Prince William Proposed to Kate," November 20, 2010. www.dailymail.co.uk/news/article-1331191/Prince-William-proposed-Kate-Middleton-remote-Kenyan-hut.html.

Chapter 4: At Home with the Cambridges

34. Quoted in Richard Kay. "He Wobbled over Kate. Now Wills Is Wobbling over a Choice That'll Define His Life." *MailOnline*, May 30, 2014. www.dailymail.co.uk/femail/article-2644414/He-wobbled-Kate-Now-Wills-wobbling-choice-thatll-define-life.html.
35. Quoted in Price. *Prince William: A Biography*, p. 145.
36. Quoted in Rebecca English. "Kate in an Afro Wig. Wills as a White Van Man. What They REALLY Got Up To at Their Anglesey Love Nest." *MailOnline*, September 22, 2013. www.dailymail.co.uk/femail/article-2429698/What-Prince-William-Kate-REALLY-got-Anglesey-love-nest.html.
37. Quoted in Katie Nicholl. "Royal Catwalk." *Vanity Fair*, September 2012. www.vanityfair.com/society/2012/09/kate-middletons-married-life-house-facials.
38. Quoted in Rebecca English. "It's Hockey in High Heels for Kate as Duchess Goes Back to Prep School She Adored." *MailOnline*, November 30, 2012. www.daily

mail.co.uk/femail/article-2240964/Duchess-Cambridge-Kate-Middleton-plays-hockey-high-heels.html.
39. Quoted in Jordan Baker. "The Duchess of Cambridge Made Being a Princess Look Easy but the Royal Tour Was Less Demanding than Those of Decades Ago." *Daily Telegraph* (Sydney, Australia), April 27, 2014. www.dailytelegraph.com.au/news/nsw/the-duchess-of-cambridge-made-being-a-princess-look-easy-but-the-royal-tour-was-less-demanding-than-those-of-decades-ago-writes-jordan-baker/story-fni0cx12-1226896870407?nk=12519899563a3ae11a1d01726e91f2c5.
40. Quoted in *Huffington Post*. "Kate Middleton Topless Photos: Nude Images of the Duchess of Cambridge Published in French Magazine *Closer* (POLL)," September 14, 2012. www.huffingtonpost.com/2012/09/14/kate-middleton-topless-photos-closer_n_1883230.html.
41. Quoted in *MailOnline*. "If the Paparazzi Could See Her, Why Couldn't Her Bodyguards See Them? Questions Raised over Failure by Royal Protection Police Just Weeks After Harry Scandal," September 14, 2012. www.dailymail.co.uk/news/article-2203485/duchess-Cambridge-topless-photos-Failure-royal-protection-police-weeks-Prince-Harry-Vegas-scandal.html.
42. Quoted in BBC News. "Kate and William: Duchess Pregnant, Palace Says," December 3, 2012. www.bbc.com/news/uk-20586343.
43. Quoted in Victoria Murphy. "'There'll Be Fireworks at the Palace': Prince William Furious at Cruel Hoax on Nurses Treating Kate." *Mirror*, December 6, 2012. www.mirror.co.uk/news/uk-news/kate-middleton-prank-call-prince-1475441.
44. Quoted in Zach Seemayer. "The Woman Behind Kate Middleton's Maternity Style." *ET* Online, September 13, 2013. www.etonline.com/fashion/138089_Interview_With_Kate_Middleton_Maternity_Designer.
45. Quoted in Max Foster and Nick Thompson. "Prince William Interview: Future King Talks Fatherhood, Baby George." CNN World, August 19, 2013. www.cnn

.com/2013/08/19/world/prince-william-interview.

46. Quoted in Foster and Thompson. "Prince William Interview."
47. Quoted in Victoria Murphy. "Diamond Jubilee: The Queen and Kate Middleton's Precious Relationship." *Mirror*, January 31, 2012. www.mirror.co.uk/news/uk-news/diamond-jubilee-the-queen-and-kate-middletons-659080.

Chapter 5: Philanthropy and Royal Duties

48. Quoted in *DNA India*. "Kate Middleton's the New Cheerleader for Britain at Olympics," August 11, 2012. www.dnaindia.com/entertainment/report-kate-middletons-the-new-cheerleader-for-britain-at-olympics-1726823.
49. Quoted in Victoria Murphy. "Royal Summer of Sport: Kate, William and Harry's Non-Stop Olympics Agenda Revealed." *Mirror*, July 5, 2012. www.mirror.co.uk/news/uk-news/kate-middleton-prince-william-and-prince-1133158.
50. Quoted in Costas Pitas. "Baby Boy George Gives Boost to Royal Family's Status." *Fiscal Times*, July 24, 2013. www.thefiscaltimes.com/Articles/2013/07/24/Baby-Boy-George-Gives-Boost-to-Royal-Familys-Status.
51. Quoted in Oliver Pickup. "Prince William Brightens Spirits by Visiting Site of Christchurch Earthquake a Month on from 'Darkest Day in New Zealand History.'" *MailOnline*, March 18, 2011. www.dailymail.co.uk/news/article-1367113/Prince-William-visits-Christchurch-worst-earthquake-New-Zealands-history.html.
52. Quoted in Candace Sutton and Rebecca English. "Dying Baby Moves Kate and William to Tears: Royal Couple Meet Little Boy the Same Age as George at Sydney Children's Hospice." *MailOnline*, April 18, 2014. www.dailymail.co.uk/news/article-2607560/Im-ready-big-sob-admits-emotional-Kate-playing-seriously-ill-children-meeting-families-hospice-Sydney.html.
53. Quoted in Susannah Palk. "Prince William: Following in His Mother's Charitable Footsteps." CNN World,

April 9, 2011. www.cnn.com/2011/WORLD/europe/04/08/william.diana.charity.work.

54. Quoted in Rachel Elbaum. "Duchess Kate's Choice of Charities Echoes Diana's." *Today*, January 5, 2012. www.today.com/id/45882658/ns/today-today_news/t/duchess-kates-choice-charities-echoes-dianas/#.U_NMiWMo3Wg.
55. Quoted on the website of the Royal Foundation of the Duke and Duchess of Cambridge and Prince Harry. www.royalfoundation.com.
56. Quoted in Ben Beaumont-Thomas. "Jon Bon Jovi and Taylor Swift Team Up with Prince . . . William." *Guardian*, November 27, 2013. www.theguardian.com/music/2013/nov/27/prince-william-sings-with-jon-bon-jovi-taylor-swift.
57. Quoted in Claudia Joseph. "Wills Decides Being a Royal WON'T Be His Full Time Job as He Opts to Become a Pilot with East Anglia Air Ambulance to Be Closer to Home." *Mail* Online, June 21, 2014. www.dailymail.co.uk/news/article-2664596/Wills-decides-Royal-WONT-time-job-opts-pilot-East-Anglia-air-ambulance-closer-home.html.
58. Robert Jobson. "Prince William Does It His Way." *Newsweek*, March 21, 2014. www.newsweek.com/prince-william-does-it-his-way-232412.
59. Graham Smith. "Why UK Should Abolish Its 'Failed' Monarchy." CNN, June 1, 2012. www.cnn.com/2012/05/30/world/europe/uk-jubilee-republicans/index.html.

Important Dates

1982

Catherine Elizabeth Middleton is born January 9 in Reading, Berkshire, England.

Prince William Arthur Philip Louis of Wales is born June 21 in London.

1997

Princess Diana dies of injuries from a car crash in Paris. Her sons, William and Harry, walk behind her casket in the funeral procession.

2001

William Wales and Catherine Middleton enroll at the University of St. Andrews in Scotland and move into the same residence hall.

2002

Kate Middleton catches William's eye on the catwalk during a charity fashion show at the University of St. Andrews.

William, Kate, and two other roommates move in together to a flat close to the St. Andrews campus.

2004

Photographers capture a kiss between William and Kate at the Klosters ski resort in Switzerland.

2005

William and Kate graduate from the University of St. Andrews.

2006

William completes a training program at the Royal Military Academy Sandhurst and is commissioned as an officer in the Household Cavalry.

2007

In mid-April, reporters announce that William and Kate have broken up after five years of dating.

Princes William and Harry host a concert on July 1 to honor the ten-year anniversary of Diana's death; Kate attends and is confirmed to be back together with William.

2010

William proposes to Kate in Kenya, Africa, in October.

2011

William and Kate get married in London on April 29 and become the Duke and Duchess of Cambridge, as well as other titles.

William and Kate go to Canada on their first royal tour together as a married couple.

2012

Photos of Kate sunbathing topless are published in a French magazine, causing controversy.

The royal family announces that Kate is pregnant.

2013

Kate gives birth to Prince George Alexander Louis of Cambridge on July 22.

In August, William announces he is retiring from military service as a search-and-rescue helicopter pilot.

William, Kate, and baby George move into Kensington Palace in London.

2014

William accepts a job in the private sector as an air ambulance helicopter pilot.

2015

William and Kate welcome their second child, Princess Charlotte Elizabeth Diana, on May 2.

For More Information

Books

Christopher P. Andersen. *William and Kate: A Royal Love Story*. New York: Gallery, 2011. An experienced biographer describes the separate lives of William and Kate before they met and their relationship after.

Katie Nicholl. *Kate: The Future Queen*. Philadelphia: Weinstein, 2013. Tells the story of Catherine Middleton, from her early life to her experiences as a duchess and royal mother.

Penny Junor. *Prince William: The Man Who Will Be King*. New York: Pegasus, 2012. A royal biographer tells the history of Prince William, from his childhood and upbringing to his marriage to a country girl.

The Royal Wedding of Prince William and Kate Middleton: Expanded, Commemorative Edition. New York: LIFE Books, 2011. Describes, with full-color photographs, the engagement and wedding of William and Catherine.

Videos

Prince William and Catherine: A Royal Love Story. (Maureen Goldthorpe, director. Needham, MA: Echo Bridge Entertainment, 2011.) This seventy-minute documentary tells the story of Prince William and Catherine Middleton's relationship and engagement with behind-the-scenes footage of their life behind and outside of castle walls.

"Take a Tour of Kate Middleton's Hometown." *Time*. http://content.time.com/time/video/player/0,32068,918270772001_2067572,00.html. This short video from *Time* magazine tours the English country town Kate Middleton called home as a child.

"William and Kate: Interview in Full." BBC News UK, November 16, 2010. www.bbc.com/news/uk-11770175. Includes footage of the first interview with Prince William and Kate Middleton after they officially announced their engagement. They discuss their relationship and hopes for the future.

Internet Sources

William Lee Adams. "Royal Revolution: Top 10 Ways William and Kate's Wedding Breaks the Mold." *Time*, April 7, 2011. http://content.time.com/time/specials/packages/0,28757,2062700,00.html.

Anthony Bond. "Pictured: Inside Kate and William's Kensington Palace Home Which Is Set for £4m Refurbishment." *Mirror*, June 21, 2014. www.mirror.co.uk/news/uk-news/pictured-inside-kate-williams-kensington-3737810.

"CNN's Prince William Interview: The Full Transcript." CNN World, August 19, 2013. www.cnn.com/2013/08/19/world/prince-william-transcript.

Jessica Derschowitz. "Prince George Turns 1: Look Back at the Future King's Memorable First Year." CBS News, July 22, 2014. www.cbsnews.com/news/prince-george-turns-1-future-king-memorable-year.

"In Pictures: Catherine Middleton's Childhood Home." *Forbes*, April 5, 2011. www.forbes.com/2011/04/05/catherine-middleton-home-royal-wedding-forbeslife_slide_3.html.

"Kate and William Arrive in Los Angeles for US Trip." *Today.com*, July 8, 2011. www.today.com/id/43681124/ns/today-today_news/t/kate-william-arrive-los-angeles-us-trip/#.VAJmSmMXOkI.

Shiv Malik. "Prince William Leaves RAF to Pursue Charity Work." *Guardian* (Manchester, UK), September 12, 2013. www.theguardian.com/uk-news/2013/sep/12/prince-william-leaves-raf-charity-work.

"Memorable Moments in Prince George's First Year." *Vanity Fair*, July 29, 2014. www.vanityfair.com/style/photos/2014/08/prince-george-photos.

Katie Nicholl. "Wills and the Real Girl." *Vanity Fair*, December 2010. www.vanityfair.com/society/features/2010/12/william-and-kate-201012.

Tim Walker. "Prince William and Kate Middleton Take On a More Active Charity Role." *The Telegraph* (UK), December 21, 2013. www.telegraph.co.uk/news/uknews/theroyalfamily/10531655/Prince-William-and-Kate-Middleton-take

-on-more-active-charity-role.html.

"What Will Prince William's Duties as an East Anglian Air Ambulance Pilot Be?" *The Guardian* (UK), August 7, 2014. www.theguardian.com/uk-news/2014/aug/07/prince-william-daily-duties-air-ambulance-pilot-east-anglia.

Websites

CNN: Complete Coverage on Royal Wedding 2011 (www.cnn.com/SPECIALS/2011/royal.wedding). A CNN site that provides links to stories and video footage on all aspects of the wedding of William and Kate.

The Commonwealth (www.thecommonwealth.org). Describes the role and mission of the British Commonwealth (currently headed by Queen Elizabeth and the royal family), lists its member countries, and describes Commonwealth goals and work throughout the world.

The Duke and Duchess of Cambridge (www.dukeandduchessofcambridge.org). Includes the latest news, photos, a blog, and a list of recent and upcoming activities, appearances, and engagements for the duke, duchess, and Prince George.

Kate Middleton's Amazing Fashion Evolution (http://content.time.com/time/photogallery/0,29307,2065084,00.html). This *Time* magazine site provides nearly a hundred photos of the duchess's most famous fashion moments.

Kate Middleton Style Blog (http://katemiddletonstyle.org). Describes some of Kate's most famous outfits and accessories, from casual to formal, and gives details of how to copy each look.

Official Website of the British Monarchy (www.royal.gov.uk). Gives historical details of the royal family as well as biographical information for all current royal family members, including William and Kate.

***People* Magazine Celebrity Central: Kate Middleton** (www.people.com/people/Kate-Middleton). Lists information about the life of Kate Middleton by decade and includes recent news about the duchess and her current activities.

Royal Family History (www.britroyals.com). Provides biographical information and family trees for British royals from the year 879 to the present.

The Royal Foundation of the Duke and Duchess of Cambridge and Prince Harry (www.royalfoundation.com). Lists the duke and duchess's fund-raising and charity news, describes sponsored causes and charities, and gives financial details and contact/donating information.

Index

Picture Credits

Cover: © Samir Hussein/WireImage/Getty Images
© Alice Dore/AFP/Getty Images, 26
© Anwar Hussein/Hulton Archive/Getty Images, 13
© AP Images/Alastair Grant, 34–35
© AP Images/Jeff J. Mitchell, 20
© Arthur Edwards/WPA Pool/Getty Images Entertainment/Getty Images, 51
© Arthur Edwards/WPA Pool/Getty Images News/Getty Images, 59
© Celia Peterson/arabianEye/Getty Images, 28–29
© Daily Mail/Rex/Alamy, 30
© Dave J. Hogan/Centrepoint/Getty Images Entertainment/Getty Images, 80
© David Cheskin/AFP/Getty Images, 44
© DEA/W. BUSS/DeAgostini/Getty Images, 66–67
© Graham Barclay/BWP Media/Getty Images News/Getty Images, 41
© James Devaney/FilmMagic/Getty Images, 53
© John Stillwell/AFP/Getty Images, 58
© John Stillwell/WPA Pool/Getty Images Entertainment/Getty Images, 64
© Julian Parker/UK Press/Getty Images, 14–15
© Leon Neal/AFP/Getty Images, 62
© Mark Cuthbert/UK Press/Getty Images, 43
© Mark Large/WPA Pool/Getty Images News/Getty Images, 76
© Mark Taylor/Getty Images Entertainment/Getty Images, 74–75
© Pascal Le Segretain/Getty Images Entertainment/Getty Images, 71
© Pool/Tim Graham Photo Library/Getty Images, 45, 49
© Richard Pohle/AFP/Getty Images, 78
© Samir Hussein/WireImage/Getty Images, 72
© Stefan Rousseau/AFP/Getty Images, 32
© Tim Graham/Tim Graham Photo Library/Getty Images, 9, 18
© Toby Melville/Newsmakers/Hulton Archive/Getty Images, 23

About the Author

Jenny MacKay has written more than twenty-five books for teens and tweens on topics ranging from crime scene investigation and sports science to social issues, world religions, and pop culture. She lives in Sparks, Nevada, with her husband, daughter, and son.